How did a ship com  the desert? Was it a Gal ? A Viking ship?

THE MYSTERIOUS WEST

SUDDEN AND UNEXPLAINED DEATHS

BURIED TREASURES AND LOST MISSIONS

ELABORATE HOAXES

HAUNTED HOUSES AND GHOST TOWNS

STRANGE CURSES   MYSTERIOUS LEGACIES

NOTORIOUS LADIES, BLOODTHIRSTY BANDITS

BEHEADINGS   CONFIDENCE SCHEMES

TALL TALES COME TRUE

The Mysterious West

Brad Williams
&
Choral Pepper

BALLANTINE BOOKS • NEW YORK
An Intext Publisher

BALLANTINE BOOKS, INC.
101 Fifth Avenue, New York, N.Y. 10003

This book is dedicated to
all those people who believe a little
bit in everything

Contents

This book is dedicated to
all those people who believe a little
bit in everything.

Preface

There is a story told of the Second World War in which a
sailor, serving on board a submarine, was stricken with appen-
dicitis. The submarine put into a small harbor of a remote
island in the South Pacific, where the sailor was transferred to
a helicopter and flown to a distant hospital ship.

The incident was witnessed by two natives who had crossed
to this uninhabited side of the island to fish. When they
returned to their village later in the day, they told of their
incredible adventure. A huge fish, they said, rose from the
bottom of the ocean, and two strangely dressed men, carrying
a third, emerged from an opening in the back of the fish.
There then appeared a most peculiar bird of immense size.
With the most raucous cry the bird slowly settled down over

the back of the fish, whereupon two of the oddly dressed men stuffed the body of the third into the open belly of the bird. The two men then climbed back into the fish, which sank into the sea, and the huge bird flew away with its victim.

The wise men of the village listened to the tale, then scoffed at such a preposterous story. Everyone knew that fish did not feed birds. It was another matter altogether. Birds ate fish. Fish did not have openings in the middle of their backs, birds did not have openings in the middle of their bellies, and in addition there never was a bird large enough to swallow a man. The two fishermen knew this was true, as did all the other residents of the village, and they respected the wise men who were the leaders. When they could not think of a logical explanation for what they had seen, they agreed with the wise men that the incident had never happened.

A parallel can be drawn between the experiences of the two native fishermen and many of the stories in this book. Everyone knows, for example, that Christopher Columbus discovered America, and thus there could not be any authentic Phoenician writings on a stone in New Mexico, nor could there have been a Roman colony near what is now Tucson, Arizona. Everyone knows that Cabrillo was the first conquistador to sail up the west coast of California, and thus the grave of a predecessor must be a hoax. Everyone knows that a multimillionaire cannot vanish and not have the incident reported in a single newspaper.

Yet behind every hoax there must be some reason—a joke or a fraud. Thus, when there is no apparent reason for a hoax, those who arbitrarily identify it as such, because it is not logical or because it differs with historical conceptions, are behaving in a most illogical manner. This book tells of some of these mysteries, labeled as hoaxes by certain wise men, who, nevertheless, have been unable to offer any reason for the hoax. It tells also of hoaxes over which there can be no doubt as to the motivation, hoaxes so grand in scope as to make by comparison the sale of the Brooklyn Bridge appear as petty larceny.

The writers have avoided deliberately the countless tales of lost treasure so common in legends of the West; stories in which a prospector expires in the arms of a close friend seconds before he can gasp out the location to a vast fortune that only he knows. Many books have covered these stories adequately. Lost treasure is discussed only where there is new positive evidence that such treasure did indeed exist, or where, in their research for this volume, the writers have uncovered an almost definite answer to the legend, as in the case of the lost black gold of the ubiquitous Peg Leg Smith, or the whereabouts of the lost Santa Isabel Mission.

The West referred to in the title of this book includes the geographical area that encompasses the western portion of the North American continent.

The authors are indebted to many persons who gave freely of their time to help in preparation of this book. These include: Thomas Bent of San Diego, California, Jim Smith of San Ignacio, Baja, California, Dr. Joseph J. Markey of Oceanside, California, Mrs. Louis Botts of Julian, California, Miss Margaret Sparks of Tucson, Arizona, Peter Damele of Austin, Nevada, Norman Wallace of Phoenix, Arizona, Estelle Latta of Sacramento, California, George T. Davis of San Francisco, California, Charles Hillinger of Los Angeles, California, Edwin J. Smart of Aspen, Colorado, Sid Smith of Jackson, California, Patrice Manahan of Los Angeles and many others.

Brad Williams
Choral Pepper
Palm Desert, California
April, 1967

1

The Arizona Romans

The face of the earth is a graveyard. In one form or another, it buries all things. Those things that have lived on the generosity of the earth are reclaimed after death to form the elements to be borrowed by future generations. Those inanimate things, made by living things, are scattered in the graveyard also. Most are ingested, but many remain to turn up in unexpected places, often causing embarrassment to dogmatic historians who decry the discovery as a hoax because it does not conform to historically accepted ideas. As we will discover later, many times the discoveries are hoaxes, such as the unearthing of a diamond mine on a Rocky Mountain mesa.

Sometimes these relics offer evidence of what previously had been considered no more than a delightful or poignant legend. Such a case is the story of Machu Picchu, the legend told of the removal of all Incan maidens from the empire cities to a hidden village high in the Andes in order to spare them from the passion of advancing conquistadores. Those Incans aware of the removal were slaughtered by the Spaniards, and the virgins, guarded only by a few aging soldiers, died of starvation in their lofty hiding place. The name of this hidden city, according to legend, was Machu Picchu, and as recently as 1910, a prominent American historian published an article in which he referred to the mythical city by name. The following year, the ruins of Machu Picchu were discovered by the American explorer Hiram Bingham. Today they may be seen with little difficulty by any visitor to Peru.

1

The legend of Machu Picchu has now been accepted as probable historical fact.

Approximately thirteen years after Bingham offered physical evidence to a legend, the earth cast up evidence of a historical incident to which there is no known record or legend. This discovery has confounded historians, many of whom have angrily decried the find as a hoax. Others remain nonplused. The place where this find was made is near an old stagecoach stop known as Nine Mile Water Hole on the fringe of Tucson, Arizona.

In the fall of 1924, Charles Manier took a visiting relative on a tour of the desert around his native Tucson and eventually arrived at Nine Mile Water Hole. In an area known as the high desert, crumbled ruins of the stagestops and old rock walls ramble across the flat mesa between thick stands of mesquite and greasewood. The air is always clear, and the sky is a deep Parrish blue, except for those days when heavy clouds bank against the distant and forbidding Pajarito Mountains and send their heavy rains into the Tucson Valley.

Along the road to Nine Mile Water Hole are the ruins of five cylindrically-shaped structures made of brick. Like many cities of the Southwest desert, where lumber was scarce and expensive, the buildings of early Tucson were made of adobe. This is a special mud that, when mixed with straw, can be dried and hardened into bricks used for construction. During occasional desert rains, adobe brick erodes into mud if not protected by a roof or outer coating of plaster. The cylindrical brick ruins near Nine Mile Water Hole are the remains of old kilns where lime used for the protective plaster was made. It was near one of these kilns that Charles Manier parked his car and, with his companion, climbed up a steep road bank for a closer inspection of the ruin.

Manier's companion carried a steel-tipped cane. Near the top of the bank he paused and leaned on his stick to catch his breath. When he again lifted the cane, it struck something metallic protruding from the wall of the bank. Curious, he tapped the object again, and again he was rewarded with the sound of metal striking metal.

In 1924, there were few paved roads around Tucson, and shovels and other digging devices were as necessary to an automobile's tool complement as a wheel jack. Thus it was but a matter of moments befort Manier was digging into the ground with a small pickaxe and trench shovel. The excavation of the object, however, took a considerably longer time, and when it finally was excavated, Manier saw only a flat, diamond-shaped polygon heavily encrusted with dirt and a rough substance. He hacked away at the tough *caliche* with his pick, working at the project for almost an hour before he recognized the object as a large religious cross made of lead which later, when weighed, was sixty-two pounds.

Manier did not consider it a startling find. Spanish conquistadores and Jesuit missionaries had crisscrossed this section of the world countless times. There was at least one lost mission reportedly in the wilderness of the Pajarito Mountains and another, well known, founded by Father Kino. Manier climbed to the top of the bank to see if there was any evidence of a small chapel. The upward slope to the rear of the hill was gentle; the apex of the ridge long and low. Shallow washes indented the terrain, but the slope on which he had made his discovery had not been caused by a water run-off. The draw had been made artificially because of the road bed cut into the natural grade of the land. Nearby was a partially completed dwelling which Manier recalled was the property of a young Tucson attorney named Thomas Bent who was homesteading eighty acres in the vicinity. Manier knew Bent casually. They were both members of a veterans' organization in Tucson, and Manier thought it would be a friendly gesture to take the cross back to Tucson and give it to the lawyer.

At first, Thomas Bent was only mildly curious about the find, for he also was aware of the ubiquitous Jesuits, although he did wonder idly why the cross was made of lead. A few days later, with the help of Manier, he cleaned the relic more thoroughly and made an intriguing discovery. Instead of one cross, there were two, of identical design fastened together with lead rivets. Carefully, Bent pried them apart. The inside of the crosses was flat, and each side was coated with a waxlike substance. A piece of the wax on one side had flaked away during the separation of the icon, and in the bared spot Bent detected what appeared to be a form of writing cut into the soft metal. Wih considerably more care, Ben and Manier scraped away the wax to reveal writing on both crosses and on both the horizontal and vertical sections.

A few days later, Bent took them to the University of Arizona where the language was identified as a form of Latin by Dr. Frank H. Fowler. The story secreted between these two

lead crosses, when translated by Dr. Fowler, was as startling
as it was incredible.

In the year 775 A.D., the story recounted, a fleet of ships
carrying about seven hundred Roman men and women under
the leadership of Theodorus the Renowned set sail from
Rome, passed through the Straits of Hercules, and immediately ran into a series of heavy storms. When the storms
subsided, there was no sign of land, and the ships that still
floated sailed together for many weeks before land was
sighted. The survivors abandoned their ships and set forth on
foot toward the northwest, another journey that was to take
many weeks and during which they were threatened contin-
ually by wild terrain, wild natives, and wild animals. Eventually the remaining members of the expedition reached a warm
desert where there was ample water supply. It was here Theodorus decided to settle permanently and build a city named
Terra Calalus. In the ensuing months, natives known as Toltezus were captured and forced into slavery. Terra Calalus
grew into a city but was razed to the ground after fourteen
years when the Indian slaves revolted and killed Theodorus.

The survivors rebuilt Terra Calalus, this time under the
leadership of a man named Jacobus, and again the labor was
supplied by enslaved Toltezus. Jacobus was succeeded by a
leader named Israel, who in turn was followed by seven more
of the same name who ruled for a total of 125 years. Then
the natives again revolted, and it was Israel VII who, when
his battle weapon was shattered by a stone axe, ordered that
the story of Terra Calalus be inscribed on the lead cross.

It sounded like a tale out of Bullfinch's *Mythology*. Bent
and Fowler were justifiably skeptical. Karl Ruppert of the
Arizona State Museum studied the translations and the lead
crosses with readily expressed bewilderment, then accompanied Manier and Bent back to the site of the discovery. The
three men dug carefully into the slope of the barranca and
presently uncovered another object which, when the *caliche*
was chipped away, disclosed a large circular piece of metal
upon which a Roman head had been engraved. The idea of
a "plant" or a hoax began to fade. Even an unskilled eye
could see that countless years had passed since the Roman
head had been buried in this undisturbed grave.

Nevertheless, the three men decided to keep their discoveries secret until an expert opinion could be obtained on the
authenticity of the artifacts. The cross and the Roman head

were stored in Bent's safe in his Tucson office to await the return from Mexico of Dr. Byron Cummings, one of the more prominent archeologists of the nation who then was on the staff of the University of Arizona.

When Cummings examined the artifacts, he too was non-plused. Immediately, he organized a small "dig" in the area of Bent's homestead. To keep the discovery quiet until scientific judgment could be passed upon its relative worth, few persons were employed in the excavation, and the working-men had their salaries paid by Bent. During the first months of the excavation, twenty-seven artifacts were discovered. These consisted of additional lead crosses, nine swords of ancient Latin design, a crescent-shaped cross, a labarum, and the engraved Roman head. Many more inscriptions, but curiously, in addition to the Latin, several words in Hebrew were included.

Assays and analyses were made of the metal. All but two were composed of a natural alloy of local origin containing lead and antimony with traces of tin, gold, and silver. The two exceptions, both articles of superior workmanship, contained copper which was classified as similar to an ore found in Arizona.

Eventually, Cummings carried the artifacts to other scholars, seeking their opinions and advice. They were tested by government experts for radioactivity. Lead alloys usually possess radioactivity when first prepared, but with age, this disappears. No trace of radioactivity was found. Microscopic tests performed on the artifacts indicated "antiquity" but no dating of the objects could be determined. Carbon-14 tests, presently used for determining age, were then unknown, but even today they would prove ineffective, as no contemporary living matter occurred in strata with the artifacts. (A Carbon-14 test is a method by which archeologists are able to measure the extent of decay in wood, bone, or any other organic matter by radioactivity, thus arriving at the approximate date when the organism was living matter.)

The most baffling aspect was the mixture of Hebrew and Latin. The Latin, a type used for records and religious inscriptions up to the eighth century, was interspersed with Jewish ecclesiastical symbols and phrases. On one artifact a knowledge of Freemasonry was indicated by a square and compass design. On a labarum, there appeared a crown resembling a patriarch's cap; the patriarch's cross with double

bars, a Roman temple with pillars and drawn swords and ser-
pent. Latin phrases such as "We are carried forward on the
sea to an unknown land," and "Nothing except peace was
sought," indicate an attempt to record history. The Hebrew
phrases suggest little more than a possible religious integration.

The testing and slowly widening awareness of the discoveries no longer could be kept secret. In July of 1925, a
reporter for the New York *Times* came to Arizona and interviewed Cummings. The results of the interview and the incredible discovery, published in a long front-page story in the
newspaper, immediately touched off a controversy that rico-
cheted from one scientist to another around the world. The
consensus was that the artifacts were an elaborate hoax, and,
according to the debunker's bias, the perpetrators ranged from
the Mormons to the Jesuits. The most vocal of the critics
were those who knew the least about it. On a regional scale,
Bent and Manier were singled out as the culprits.

Dr. Cummings, whose integrity could not be challenged and
whose position in archeological circles was most secure, called
a press conference to answer the critics. All of the relics, he
said, had been found encased in a solid, undisturbed strata of
tough *caliche,* some as much as six feet below the surface of
the ground. This alone precluded any possibility of a hoax,
unless it had been concocted prior to the arrival of Christopher Columbus. "These Roman artifacts are unequivocably
authentic," he stated.

Whether or not they were as ancient as A.D. 900, the date
indicated on the labarum—the imperial standard of the later
Roman emperors—he would not say, but he added that they
had been in their graves for many, many years before the
arrival of the Spanish conquistadores. The evidence of this
was irrefutable, he said, not only because of the undisturbed
condition of the *caliche,* but also because of the discovery in
the same area and depth from the surface of a pueblo culture
at least eight hundred years old.

His assertions, however, failed to convince the skeptics,
including Dr. Fowler who had made the first translations.
What disturbed this classical scholar was the discovery that
some of the Latin phrases inscribed on the artifacts were
similar to phrases used in two Latin grammar books long out
of print. Although the phrasing was similar, the spelling was
different, but this was sufficient to place Dr. Fowler on the
side of the unbelievers.

By no means, however, was Cummings alone in his belief as to the authenticity of the relics. Dean G. M. Butler of the College of Mines and Engineering at the University of Arizona made public the results of his study. "The objects were introduced into the *caliche* before cementation with the calcium carbonate occurred," he declared. "Accumulation comes as a result of a very slow process. There is no chance that the objects were introduced into the *caliche* formation during the time Americans had occupied this section of the country."

A retired Mexican cattleman named Leandro Ruiz next offered his solution to the mystery. When Maximilian was placed on the Mexican throne by Napoleon, many Mexicans fled the country as political exiles. Among them was the family of Timitio Odohui. Prior to his flight, Odohui had been an upper-class metallurgist, but while in exile, he had been reduced to working at the lime kilns near Nine Mile Water Hole in Arizona. Odohui had a son, according to Ruiz, who not only was adept at sculpture, but also possessed an extensive library which consisted of books on classical literature and ancient history. In addition, Ruiz reported, the son, Vincente, was enamored with tales of buried treasure. Because of Vincente's talent, his knowledge and his habitat, Ruiz told newsmen, the existence of the artifacts probably could be traced to the son of the political exile.

Ruiz' story attracted considerable attention. Newsmen went hunting for Vincente who, with his mother, had moved away from Nine Mile Water Hole shortly after his father's death. The search was dropped, however, when both Cummings, Butler, and other prominent scholars reminded the public that even the most talented sculptor would have been unable to age a relic in *caliche*.

The controversy waned. There were those who believed, and those who did not believe. When the pros and cons were exhausted, the news media lost interest and turned its attention elsewhere. For two years, Bent and Manier continued their excavations under the guidance of Cummings. Such digging, however, not only is tiresome but also expensive. During the week, Bent maintained his law practice in Tucson, good-naturedly accepting the jibes from his neighbors for his "folly." On weekends, he went back to his homestead with his shovel and screens. While he practiced law, he employed men to continue the search on his property.

Early in 1927, with the help of Cummings, Bent entered

into a contract with the University of Arizona. The terms called for the university to reimburse Bent and Manier for their two years of work in conducting the excavation, and it also gave them permission to display the Roman relics in the Arizona State Museum until such time as their authenticity could be established. Before the contract could be consummated, however, the university hierarchy was turned over completely, including its president. Cummings became director of the Arizona State Museum, and the new university administrators canceled the pending contract on the grounds that too much commercialism was creeping into the affair.

The artifacts, at this writing, are stored in an Arizona vault. The site of Terra Calalus is fenced and a sign warns passersby of the penalty they face if caught trespassing. Cummings is dead; so is Manier. Thomas Bent, now retired, lives with his wife in San Diego, California, still the legal owner of Arizona's ancient Roman townsite. He has the lawyer's logical attitude toward the artifacts, the same attiude he has maintained since the day Manier first brought the leaded double cross to his home in Tucson. He neither believes nor disbelieves in their authenticity. He merely seeks definite proof for either possible answer, although he admits wryly that if he had it to do over again he might follow the action of the aged Mexican watchman whom he hired when the excavations were in progress. The watchman told Bent that he had worked in the kilns when he was a youth and that he had found an old sword buried in the area.

"What did you do with it?" Bent asked.

"I gave it to some kids to play with," the watchman replied, with a shrug.

Cummings was ninety-six years old when he died in 1954. Shortly before his death, he paid his last visit to the site of Terra Calalus and took time to reminisce with Frank Howard, who now lives in the house on the original Bent homestead. There is a strong possibility, he told Howard, that the relics had been carried by the victorious Indians to the site where they were found and then later, after interest in their spoils of war declined, had been abandoned as worthless souvenirs.

Ignoring Cummings' opinion, and Bent's neutral stand, there are many qualified persons in the United States who see nothing to scoff at in the discovery. As recently as 1966, a spokesman for the Archeological Society of Brigham Young University at Provo, Utah, wrote: "What seems to have happened, if the artifacts are genuine—and I see no reason to suppose they are not—is that some group, perhaps from the Mediterranean area, with a knowledge of both Christianity and Hebrew, intruded itself into the American Southwest somewhere around 700 to 800 A.D. The fact that the Latin inscriptions do not make much sense could indicate that generations had passed by and that the colony was rapidly losing its knowledge of how to write. . . . What is needed, it seems to me, is further carefully controlled field investigations by trained archaeologists with sufficient funds and facilities and a genuine interest in the problem."

The Romans certainly had the ships capable of crossing the Atlantic. Lionel Casson, who wrote *The Ancient Mariners,* reports that by 64 A.D. the Romans boasted an enormous merchant fleet. Ordinary freighters averaged 340 tons, ships of the grain fleet ran up to 1,200 tons. Flavius Josephus reported that in the year 64 he journeyed from Alexandria to Rome in a ship that carried six hundred passengers. There is a reference by the Greek historian Lucian to a Roman ship that was driven by a gale into the harbor at Athens. He described the vessel as 180 feet in length, 45 feet wide, and with a depth in her hold of 44 feet. They are a rather startling comparison to the tiny ships in which Columbus sailed across the sea several centuries later.

Roman coins have been found buried in Venezuela. Roman artifacts have been found buried near Jeffress, Virginia, . . . and a Roman colony named Terra Calalus has been found near Tucson, Arizona.

There is, however, evidence that indicates that the old Romans were not the first Europeans to roam the West. Before the Romans came the Phoenicians.

2

New Mexico's Phoenicians

In the fall of 1946, a retired Michigan State policeman appeared in the offices of the Associated Press in Albuquerque, New Mexico. He had been prospecting for uranium in the desert area some miles southwest of the city, he said, and near the top of a bluff he had seen a large rock with writing "that appeared Egyptian" chiseled into it. He was more than happy to lead a reporter and a photographer to the site.

The rock was in one of the more desolate areas of the state, yet oddly in the middle of one of New Mexico's school districts on a bluff overlooking the dry Rio Puerco River. The closest village was Los Lunas, a community obviously named by someone unfamiliar with Spanish because it ungrammatically couples a masculine article with a feminine noun. The fact that the deserted area was in a school district was due to a vagary in the New Mexican law. Many years earlier, conscientious lawmakers on a state level were determined that enough land would be set aside in the various counties of New Mexico to provide for future school expansion. In some areas, however, county officials to whom the authority of the districting had been delegated, circumvented the intent of the legislature, probably because of pressure from local interests. The reason for this pressure is open to conjecture, but because of it many counties appropriated the required acreage in the least desirable section of the county. In certain instances, such as this one, the land reserved for future school expansion was in an area so desolate that the most avaricious land grabber could not possibly voice an objection.

10

The last three miles en route to the rock were cross-country, over a flat high mesa that ended on a steep arroyo where once, many, many years earlier, a large and deep river flowed. The bluff actually was a small hill with a 45-degree grade. The marks of erosion caused by the ancient river were visible along the lower part of the hill.

The basalt rock to which the retired police officer referred was just below the crown of the hill, and the hieroglyphics had been chiseled into its basalt face. At one time, the rock probably had been perpendicular to the mesa, but over the years, the earth supporting it had slipped and now it tipped toward the slope of the hill. The chiseling did indeed appear like Egyptian writing to the reporter and the photographer. Because of the position of the rock, it was obvious that it could not have been done while the rock was in its present position. The photographer scrubbed out the dirt that had accumulated in the lines, outlined them in chalk, then wriggled underneath the boulder on his back in order to get his picture. After the photographs were taken, the trio climbed to the top of the hill where several Indian arrowheads were found.

A copy of the picture was sent by the Associated Press to the Smithsonian Institute, which reported back that the inscription was a combination of Phoenician, Hebrew, and Greek, that it recited the Ten Commandments and that its existence had been known for several years prior to its discovery by the former Michigan State policeman. In 1936, it had been examined by Dr. Frank Hibben, an anthropologist from the University of New Mexico; although it was well worn and old, the inscription probably had been carved by a Mormon during an encampment on his trek west. The translation originally had been made by Dr. Robert Pfeiffer of Harvard University.

Although there was considerable discussion in the AP bureau in Albuquerque as to how any Mormon coming from anywhere to Salt Lake City could get that far off course, the news of the find was not filed. In the remote possibility that it was the work of a passing Mormon, it is unlikely that one of these hardy pioneers would have written his proselytizing message in Phoenician and in a spot so rarely seen.

The hieroglyphics on the New Mexican rock are similar to those inscribed on the sarcophagus of the King of Sidon, which dates from about 572 B.C., even to the same combination of the three languages. Thus we have a situation whereby, if the inscription is a hoax, the desert drifter who perpetuated it more than a century ago was incredibly well informed on his Phoenician history, was willing to spend several days in a hot and remote desert setting up his hoax, carried the necessary tools needed to chisel on hard basalt, lay flat on his back on the side of a steep hill to chisel the inscription, picked a location where the odds were great that it never would be found, then departed and left no hint as to its existence.

If it is a hoax, it would require all of these suppositions. The writing is known to be at least one hundred years old. The upheaval that tipped the rock in its present position occurred at least three centuries past or more, according to geologists, and the surface of the rock is so hard that it would require a hammer and chisel to write the inscription. One side of the rock is buried so close to the ground that the writer, in order to get a one-inch swing of his hammer, would have been forced to use a chisel less than two inches long.

The channel at the foot of the hill at one time harnessed a very wide and fairly deep river. To the north, it quickly becomes narrower, then disappears under the lava flow of an extinct volcano, Mount Taylor. In the southerly direction the dry river bed continues to widen, then empties into the Rio Grande River, which once was a stream that rivaled the Mississippi in size and, like the Mississippi, travels many hundreds of miles to reach the Gulf of Mexico. It seems equally preposterous, however, to assume that the inscription is authentic; that it could have been made by some ancient Phoenician scribe—or does it?

It is well known that the Phoenicians were the great traders and sailors of the Middle East. As early as 1250 B.C., the Phoenicians and the Greeks controlled the Mediterranean. They invented the keel, which gave them control of their vessels under sail and both their merchant ships and warships were about one hundred feet long. They were a secretive race, apparently operating on the principle that a secret can best be kept if it is not written down. Most of our knowledge of Phoenicia comes from Greeks who wrote down everything they could learn about the Phoenicians. Oddly, however, the Greeks took their alphabet from the Phoenicians, and this is the same basic alphabet we use today.

The Phoenicians often chartered their merchant vessels. The Bible tells the story (I Kings, chapter 9) of one such transaction entered into between King Solomon of Israel and King

Hiram of Sidon in Phoenicia in which Solomon chartered some vessels of the Phoenician merchant fleet to bring back a shipment of silver and gold from Ophir. This was one venture in which Solomon was not very wise, for the Phoenicians, after the first delivery, sent up a regular run of their own to Ophir, diverting this source of wealth to their own coffers.

The Phoenicians founded the city of Carthage and Gades. The latter still lives today in Spain under the name of Cadiz. By the sixth century B.C., they had moved far beyond the Straits of Gibraltar. Regular trade routes were set up to Britain, and evidence has been uncovered that they had reached the island of Corvo, the westernmost island in the Azores which is approximately one thousand miles from North America. Even more amazing is the fact that they had successfully traveled around the Cape of Good Hope in Africa to open a trade route to India, according to the Greek scholar Herodotus. By 300 B.C., their ships had opened Scandinavia to commerce, and many marine historians believe that the Vikings acquired their wanderlust and inclination toward pillage from the Phoenicians. The ships of both the Vikings and the Phoenicians are of the same basic design. There are historical references relating the Phoenicians to Ultima Thule, although there is disagreement among the experts as to whether this is Norway, Iceland, or Greenland. Thus it is well established that the Phoenicians had a good understanding of navigation, possessed seaworthy ships that could circumnavigate Africa some two hundred centuries before Vasco da Gama, and roamed incessantly in search of treasure and trade.

As Charles Michael Boland points out in *They All Discovered America*, there is almost incontrovertible evidence that the Phoenicians were no strangers to the North and South American continents. Assuming Ultima Thule to be Iceland, it would be no problem for the Phoenicians to get over to North America on the comparatively short voyage. Boland tells of the Phoenician relics found at Pattee's Caves in New Hampshire, in Mechanicsburg, Pennsylvania, and even in Brazil. The Phoenician coins found on Corvo in the eighteenth century were all dated between 300 B.C. and 320 B.C.

Thus, it should not be considered presumptuous to assume that one of their ocean-going vessels sailed around the Florida Keys, up the Gulf of Mexico, and continued on up the vast river that we know today as the Rio Grande.

Near New Mexico's Phoenician Rock is approximately

where such a voyage would halt, as the stream no longer was navigable. Why some ancient Phoenician would while away his time carving out the Ten Commandments is anyone's guess —if he did.

Some may prefer the other theory; that a desert prospector or a Mormon missionary, who was an expert on Phoenician language and hieroglyphics, found a most isolated spot in the desert, where there was a rock like a low ceiling, to inscribe a message that was a hoax that he never thought worth disclosing.

It is all a part of the mysterious West.

3

From the Desert to the Sea—And Back

Long ago a great flood came to the desert and everyone was forced to move up into the hills to await the leaving of the water. Almost every year in the time of the spring there was a flood, but this was the greatest flood of all and it lasted the longest time. One day, after the third dance had been held, there appeared a great bird with white wings that moved slowly across the top of the water. It came to rest on the top of a hill that the water barely covered, and never was it able to free itself. Soon the waters went away and the great bird fell over on its side and died. The wind blew away its white wings and the body of the great bird slowly slid down the hill where soon the wind threw sand over it to bury it. Sometimes the wind blows away the sand and the body of the great bird can be seen again, but the bird is an omen of evil and harm will come to whoever draws near.

—Old Indian Legend

A few centuries past, the Colorado River was much more mighty than it is today. Almost every year when the spring runoff poured down from the distant Rocky Mountains the Colorado River alternated its course like a long wet pendulum. It knew no boundaries when it poured into the desert floor over which it must travel in its race to the Gulf of California. To a passenger on a high flying jet the desert today resembles a huge piece of wormwood, testimony to the thousands of scars left in the land by the erratic and often vicious Colorado River. There is geological evidence that, at certain times in the past, the river furrowed such a deep channel into

15

the gulf during spring rampages that salt water from the sea poured back into the channel after the floor subsided.

On the California side of the desert is the Salton Sink, the lowest area of land within the United States, some two hundred feet below sea level. Each time the sink was visited by the Colorado, it became a lake. Each time it was deprived of water, it dried up. Fossil evidence indicates that on at least two occasions in the past, the gulf broke through the delta-plain and joined it with the sea. No one knows with certainty how many times it has been filled and emptied, but the most recent inundation occurred in 1906 when the Colorado created the present Salton Sea.

These countless transitions from sand pit to sea have left many paradoxes. Grotesque concretions, like giant mushrooms, skeletons, serpents, and mythical monsters litter vast regions of the desert floor. One such area is in the Anza-Borrego State Park where there are acres upon acres of round concretions. Made up of sandstone cemented into shape with calcium carbonate, there is no dispute about their connection with bodies of water that have filled the Salton Sea. Another curious spectacle in the Salton Sink is a vast oyster-shell bed formed during one of the sink's unions with the Gulf of California. Averaging eight inches across, these petrified shells of the *Ostrea vespertina*, or ruffled oyster species, lived here about ten million years ago. In nearby areas are many thousands of tiny fresh-water shells deposited during a later epoch. Many, many years past, the sink was the bottom of a vast fresh-water body known as Lake Cahuilla, and primitive fish traps of the Indians still may be seen on the old water line of this lake a few miles south of Palm Desert. It was fed by the Colorado River and drained into the gulf, and there is a legend that the earth shook and that this huge body of water, covering hundreds of square miles, disappeared within a day and a night. All of this lends credence to the legend of an ancient ship, partially buried in sand in a desolate canyon of the California desert badlands.

One of the more intriguing versions is the story told by the Señora Petra Tucker who, before she married her prospecting husband, was the widow of one Santiago Socia. It was Santiago who first found the ancient ship of the desert. A wealthy Mexican of quick temper, he had fled Los Angeles to escape a hangman's noose. He took up residence in the border city of Tecate where he awaited the arrival of Petra. While he waited, he heard from an Indian peon that several *ollas* of gold were buried in the desert mountains of the United States about forty kilometers northeast of Tecate. The peon just happened to have a map of the gold's location, just happened to need some quick cash, and thus was willing to sell Santiago the chart. A transaction was quickly consummated. Santiago waited for Petra to arrive, then waited in Tecate for another couple of months before chancing the trip across the border to pick up his treasure. He returned a month later with no *ollas* of gold, but he told Petra a strange story.

While searching for the treasure, he had entered several canyons near the floor of the desert and in the bottom of one with high sheer walls was an ancient ship with round discs on its side. Only a portion of the ship projected from the sand. On the wall above the ship was some strange writing carved into the rock, not Indian, not English nor Spanish, nor any other language with recognizable letters. The bow of the ship was curved and carved like the long neck of a bird. Santiago had brought back a souvenir of his find, a shield made of metal in the shape of a tortilla, only larger, which was one of a series attached to the side of the ship. What happened to it? It was heavy and worthless and was thrown away. What happened to Santiago? He was a man of quick temper, and he died within a year of bullet wounds received in Sonora. The location of the strange vessel was forgotten, other than that it lies in a narrow canyon some forty kilometers northeast of Tecate.

Very recently some records were discovered concerning an official inquiry that was held by the Spanish Court in 1574 in Guadalajara. A strange fleet of vessels had been sighted sailing north in the Gulf of California. The vessels resembled Galician caravels with pelican figureheads. The fleet consisted of three large and five small vessels. Because they obviously were not of Spanish origin, the Crown had ordered an investigation. The witnesses in the investigation included Spanish soldiers and Indians who lived in pueblos along the western coast of Mexico. All described the vessels in a similar manner. One of the witnesses was a Franciscan friar who was brought up in a European seaport and familiar with the sailing vessels of many nations. Never had he seen vessels such as these.

No conclusion was reached in the investigation, nor is there any mention of a vessel of this description being seen again

—until 1933, a year remembered in southern California because of the great earthquake which leveled Long Beach, California, and caused damage for many miles around.

Myrtle and Louis Botts of Julian, California, often came down from their mountain village near San Diego to camp in the desert. Their favorite spot was near an area of natural mineral springs, some hot and some cold, which today are maintained as a resort by the United States Park Service. In the thirties, however, hardly anyone knew about Agua Caliente Springs, and it was then that the Bottses arrived with their tent and enough supplies to remain for a week.

Myrtle Botts was, and still is, the librarian in charge of the Public Library of Julian. She is also a serious amateur botanist and was one of the founders of the famous wildflower show held annually in Julian. Desert wildflowers depend entirely upon the rain that falls during early winter months. If the desert receives heavy rains in January or February, its floor will be wild with color in March. If the rains fail to materialize, the seeds are unable to germinate and must wait another year or more until the seasonal rains do fall. It was to survey the rain situation and to search for possible new specimens that the Bottses came to the remote desert area near Agua Caliente Springs in the spring of 1933.

On their second or third night out, they camped near the entrance to a deep canyon where there was a cold water spring. While preparing their supper, a dusty and semi-illiterate prospector arrived to replenish his water supply. Some days earlier, he told the Bottses, he had been well into the canyon where he had seen an old ship sticking out of some dirt right in the side of the mountain. The Bottses were interested, but the prospector could tell them nothing more, other than that the ship was "yonder up the canyon." When he told them that he also knew where the lost Peg Leg Mine was located, the Bottses dismissed him as a garrulous old man and rejected his tale of the lost ship.

The following morning the Bottses hiked into the canyon in their quest for wildflower specimens for the upcoming show. They followed the floor of the defile, eyes fastened to the ground; then, as the grade became steeper, they paused for a brief rest. Mrs. Botts noticed it first.

Jutting out of the canyon wall, almost immediately overhead, was the forward portion of a large and very ancient vessel. A curved stem head swept up from its prow. Along both sides of the vessel were clearly discernible circular marks in the wood, quite possibly left by shields which at one time had been attached to the vessel. Near the bow, on one side of the ship, were four deep furrows in the wood. The craft was high enough to hide its interior from the Bottses' view and the side of the canyon was so steep that it could be scaled only by an expert mountain climber. Indeed, he might have trouble because the wall was composed of shale and clay, too unstable to support his weight.

For a long time, the Bottses studied the curious sight, then slowly retraced their steps to their camp, taking careful note of landmarks in order to experience no difficulty in returning to the ship. The earthquake struck at almost the moment they emerged from the canyon. Both were thrown to the ground, and as they clutched the moving earth in terror, they could see their camp shaking itself to pieces in front of them. Mrs. Botts remembers their empty car bouncing across the desert floor as if it were being driven slowly over railroad ties. When the rumble had subsided and the earth once again had become calm, the Bottses retrieved their wandering automobile and gathered up their scattered camp supplies. The spring that had been cold the night before, Mrs. Botts discovered, had now become hot.

The earthquake had been a severe one, causing extensive damage in Long Beach and many other sections of southern California, but as is the case in most natural disasters, it was soon forgotten. Not forgotten by the Bottses was the strange ship in the desert canyon. Preliminary research in her library told Mrs. Botts that the vessel most nearly resembled an old Viking ship, yet she could not believe that the craft could be one of those ancient piratical vessels. Before she reported her discovery, she decided to have another look at the craft and to support her announcement with some photographs. Thus, the following weekend, the Bottses once again set out for the desert area near Agua Caliente Springs.

Once again, the couple hiked up the steep canyon, but this time when they came to the spot where they had paused to rest, their passage was blocked. Half the mountainside had fallen into the canyon, the unstable earth shaken loose by the heavy temblor. There was no sign of the ancient ship. If the earthquake had occurred a short time earlier, the Bottses realized uncomfortably, they also would have been buried under the tons of earth shaken from the mountain.

Today, Mrs. Botts is not sure what kind of an ancient ship she and her husband, and an old prospector, saw in the desert canyon. It could have been Phoenician, or it could have been Roman, but she feels that it was Viking. Eventually there will be another earthquake around Agua Caliente Springs and possibly the earth will open to display this ancient vessel.

There are other legends and tales of lost ships in the vast California desert. The Seri Indians, who live on Tiburon Island in the Gulf of Mexico, sing of one. This once hostile and murderous tribe preserves its history through song, a curious lilting monotone that is passed down through generations by tribal historians trained for their task from childhood. One song recounts the arrival of the "Came From Afar Man." Many, many years in the past there appeared at Tiburon Island a huge boat that contained many, many men with yellow hair and a woman with red hair. They remained at the island for many, many days while the men went hunting with their arrows and spears. One man, who was their chief, remained behind and lay with the red-haired woman on the boat. When the hunters returned with their game, the boat departed from the land of the Seris.

No mention is made in the song of how the visitors escaped with their lives. It was a Viking custom for captains to have their wives along. Another story in the lost-ship syndrome involves a modern Viking, one Nels Jacobsen, a rancher in California's Imperial Valley. Jacobsen reportedly found the skeleton of an ancient boat near his house some six miles east of Imperial City in 1907 and thriftily salvaged the lumber from it to build a pigpen.

There are records, however, that support the most persistent legend of a lost ship in the desert and that may have given birth to the old Indian legend of the great bird with the white wings. Thanks to the predilection of the Spaniards for forever saving anything that ever has been put on paper, the archives in Guadalajara, Mexico, tell of the experiences of a hapless young captain named Juan de Iturbe who did indeed lose his ship somewhere in the Salton Sink.

Until the end of the First World War, the tidelands of southern Baja, California, were one of the largest pearl centers of the world. Pearl-bearing oyster beds extended for miles along the Gulf Coast of Baja and it did not take long for the avaricious Spanish to learn of this treasure beneath the sea.

(The pearling industry was destroyed in 1919 when an unknown disease killed all of the oysters.)

Harvesting the pearls was closely supervised by the Spaniards. Some independent operators were licensed to work the pearl beds, but generally the harvest was reaped by salaried divers. Records were kept of the amount of the harvest, of the trials of those caught pearling illegally, of the ships of the Spanish fleet that patrolled the coast to enforce the pearling regulations, and of the occasional raids by pirates. It is among these records that the story of the young Captain Juan de Iturbe comes to light.

In 1615 de Iturbe departed San Blas in command of three ships assigned to a pearling mission off La Paz. Six months later, after a half year of exceptionally good pearling, he prepared to return to San Blas. Within an hour after his departure, his small fleet was sighted by the Dutch corsair Joris van Spielbergen who promptly captured one of the ships and removed its precious cargo. De Iturbe dispatched the other ship to warn the Manila galleon, which was due, of the corsair's presence; then, in his own ship, he fled to the north. The corsair elected to chase de Iturbe, knowing perhaps that eventually he would trap him at the head of the gulf.

However, when de Iturbe reached the end of the gulf, he found that it narrowed into a wide channel. He sailed into it on the tide and, when through, to his amazement found himself on another large sea. Charts in his possession showed clearly that Baja was a peninsula, not an island, but there wasn't a naval officer alive who didn't secretly cherish the idea that cartographers were mistaken and the legendary Straits of Anian, purported to provide a passage from the gulf to the Pacific Ocean, would turn up after all. De Iturbe convinced himself that he had found it.

He sailed north, looking for passage around the mountains on the west. At approximately 34 degrees latitude, which is the present site of the Salton Sea, he found his passage blocked. Other than for a river entering the sea, there was nothing but desert sand, a few foothills, and distant mountains. Disappointed, he turned south, but he was unable to find the wide channel to the gulf through which he had entered. In its place was a small stream, barely large enough to provide passage for a longboat. He turned back toward the north. The river that had fed this inland sea had vanished. He was landlocked. Very shortly thereafter, he ran aground.

De Iturbe abandoned his ship and its valuable cargo of pearls, hiked back to the gulf, and he and his crew eventually made their way back to Mexico.

Was de Iturbe's ship the great white bird of the Indian legend? Some historians say no. When the explorer Melchior Diaz traveled to the mouth of the Colorado in 1540, he reported no lake nor sea. More than two centuries later, when de Anza struggled through the desert seeking a land route to Upper California, the sink was still dry. Thus, say the skeptics, de Iturbe's testimony is false. His ship is not the great white bird.

It is, however, easy to answer the skeptics. Water from the Salton Sea of today evaporates in the dry desert heat at the rate of six feet per year. A lake twice the size of the present Salton Sea could have come and gone between the visits of Diaz and de Anza.

Shortly before the turn of the century, a Dr. J. P. Widney advanced a plan under which the Colorado River would be diverted intentionally into the Salton Sink. It was a beautiful idea proposed by the doctor, and it won nearly unanimous support among the newspaper editors of the times. Even the governor of Arizona made the arduous trip to Washington, D.C., in an attempt to get a Congressional appropriation to finance the project.

The proposed inland lake was named Widney Sea, and it was to stretch from the Colorado Delta, across the Mexican border more than one hundred miles north into the United States, just south of what is now Palm Springs, California. Cities such as Mexicali, Calexico, El Centro, Brawley, Mecca, and Indio would be inundated.

To Widney, the Salton Sink was nothing more than a thermal waste, "a scorched, blasted bed of some old cyclopean furnace." Under his plan, great climatic changes would occur. Southern California would enjoy a climate similar to that of the Hawaiian or Bahamian Islands. If his idea had been brought to fruition, there would be none of the temperature inversions over the Los Angeles Basin which today plague that area and result in a nearly constant smog. The skies would be washed clean of pollution by frequent heavy showers. The land would be a subtropical green rather than a desert brown.

The Los Angeles Star is typical of the newspaper support the plan received. An editorial read:

If Congress would take the matter up and appoint a scientific commission to visit the region and make a report as to the practicability, cost and effect, and should that report corroborate the view of Dr. Widney, a great country, almost a nation in itself might be reclaimed from a desert and rains be induced to fall where now a bleak and parched country is wasting away for lack of moisture.

Other newspapers demanded that the Congressional delegations from Arizona, Utah, Nevada, and California press for the appointment of such a commission. Widney devoted almost all of his time to his project.

"In western Arizona," he said, "there are traces of an ancient population much more dense, much more highly civilized than those now inhabiting this section of the country. There are ruins of cities, once large and populous, canals for extensive systems of irrigation, fragments of pottery so numerous that the ground seems paved with them." The evidence of a previous civilization, he argued, was proof that such an inland sea once had existed and that it could exist again.

There were many critics. If the climate were changed, then the dreaded disease of malaria would infect southern California. Boa constrictors and alligators would find a haven in California, posing a constant danger to the safety of women and children.

Public sentiment overwhelmingly endorsed the plan. General John C. Fremont, governor of the Arizona Territory, publicly expressed his impatience with the vacillation and dalliance of the Congress over the proposal and set out for Washington to get the plan moving. General Fremont, however, had been engaged in a long running feud with a General George Stoneman, one of the more prominent residents of Los Angeles. When Fremont departed for Washington, Stoneman could not resist the opportunity to attack his rival.

"To fill such a pond in one year would require a small stream of twenty feet wide, twenty feet deep with a current of three miles per hour," he announced in Los Angeles. "To fill such a lake, the size of Lake Erie, by a stream the size of the present Colorado River would take two hundred years. Archimedes, you know, said that he could move the world, only give him a fulcrum. Fremont says he can make a sea, only give him plenty of greenbacks."

Stoneman cited many other figures, including the rate of

evaporation, the saturation rate through the earth, and the seepage into the Gulf of California, accenting each point with a slide rule he carried in his hand. By the time he was through, he had demolished the entire project of the Widney Sea. Widney made a desperate effort to restore public sentiment for the Widney Sea plan, using several competent engineers to point out that Stoneman's "solid facts" were indeed pure fiction, but he was unsuccessful and within a few weeks the entire plan was practically forgotten.

In the spring of 1906, Stoneman's figures were most eloquently disproved. The Colorado River once again turned its attention toward the Salton Sink. Within a period of a year it filled up the lowest portion of the basin, an area about fifty miles long and ten miles across before it once again changed its course capriciously and cut another channel into the gulf east of the mountain range. So sudden was this onslaught that a string of freight cars was trapped in a siding next to the sprawling Liverpool Salt Works. The cars and the factory still remain at the bottom of the Salton Sea.

Never again will the Salton Sink be filled by a rampaging Colorado River. The stream is now well harnessed by a series of dams and pours docilely into the gulf below the Mexican-United States border. Most of the silt it used to carry sifts to the bottom of Lake Mead behind Boulder Dam. This does not mean, however, that when the Salton Sea evaporates it never again will be filled.

Below the sink is a comparatively small natural dike, an insignificant range of foothills, which holds the Gulf of California from the below-sea-level sink. Steadily it is eroding. Twice a day, the tides of the Pacific are compressed into the 700-mile-long funnel that is the gulf. At its opening, the gulf is 150 miles wide. At its top, the gulf is a mere 32 miles across. Huge tidal bores, more than ten feet high, batter this natural dike month in and month out, and every time they recede between assaults, they carry a little more of the range with them.

Before the Colorado was dammed, it carried tons of silt daily into the gulf and the silt acted as a cushion to the attack by the tidal bores. However, the Colorado River now has been tamed. Its silt drops into the lakes behind the dams, and the dike takes the full brunt of the tidal bores.

The Salton Sink will fill again. The cities of Mexicali, Calexico, El Centro, Brawley, and Indio will be inundated.

The gulf will extend northward to the cities of Palm Springs and Palm Desert. Fortune hunters in the area will be forced to seek sunken, rather than buried, treasure.

But if Dr. Widney's theories prove correct, the frequent and heavy showers over the Los Angeles Basin may forever end the air pollution problem in the City of Angels.

Even one hundred years ago, California was much more fertile than it is now. Southern California particularly is turning into a desert; indeed most of it has become a desert. Streams such as the Los Angeles River and the Rio Hondo are now little more than names, or a flood-control ditch to remove the waters from a rare shower that may occur in the winter months. Maps still show lakes that no longer exist.

One of these is Owens Lake in California's Inyo County. In 1878, however, Owens Lake was a deep body of water more than twenty miles long and ten miles wide. At one end the lake bordered the small town of Cartago, on what is now Highway 395, west of Death Valley. At the other end was the now defunct community of Keeler, a mining town for the once abundant Cerro Gordo silver mines.

Between the two towns plied a steamer some ninety feet long with the name of *Mollie Stevens*. The *Mollie Stevens* carried lumber on her decks, passengers in her cabins, and silver bullion from the Cerro Gordo mines in her hold. At Cartago, the silver was unloaded for transportation by mule train into Los Angeles.

In 1878 the *Mollie Stevens* picked up an exceptionally heavy load of bullion at Keeler and set forth for Cartago. The load was reputed to be worth more than a half million dollars. In addition to the five-man crew, there were also on board six passengers. In the middle of the lake, the steamer ran head-on into a heavy squall. The waves broke over the bow, and in a matter of a few moments, the overladen ship plunged to the bottom of the lake. So quickly did the mishap occur that the crew had no time to launch the lifeboat. One miner managed to survive by floating through the storm with the aid of a hatch cover.

By the turn of the century the tragedy of the *Mollie Stevens* was forgotten except by a few of the oldest inhabitants, and a faded two-paragraph story from the Los Angeles *Times* which was eventually preserved in the archives of the

Inyo County Museum. The story was passed around just enough to keep it alive in the tiny village of Cartago.

Over the years the lake grew smaller and smaller, eventually becoming a meadow, and then part of a sterile desert.

In December of 1961, Bob White, a pilot from Lone Pine, California, by chance was flying very low over the old lake bed, not knowing the history of the terrain below him. With him was a William Carasco and an Ed Levett, also of Lone Pine.

"There's a rock down there that looks like an old ship's propeller," Carasco said and pointed.

White circled, stared curiously, and presently landed on the flat ground near the odd rock formation. Then they saw the lifeboat with the double oarlocks. The rock formation, they discovered, was a ship's propeller. The lifeboat was so fragile it fell apart when they touched it, but they did salvage the oarlocks and the propeller, carrying both back with them in the plane to Lone Pine.

Almost a week passed before they uncovered the story of the *Mollie Stevens* and its valuable load of silver. The men have been looking ever since for the spot where they found the old prop of the *Mollie Stevens,* but at last report they have been unsuccessful.

Many years ago the boundary between California and Arizona followed the course of the Colorado River. After the boundary was determined, however, the course of the river changed and a segment of populated land about 150 miles square became the basis of a bitter controversy between the two states.

Authorities in California contended the land was theirs, as the boundary was set by the old course of the river. Arizona, however, asserted that when the river changed its course, it automatically changed the state line.

This all made life rather hectic for the few hundred souls living within the disputed area. Both states demanded property taxes and sent in collectors to garner them. Some of the residents voted in California, others in Arizona. A few years ago, a small group voted in both states on an election day in an attempt to point up their plight.

Partially as a result of this, the boundary dispute was placed on the agenda of the Federal Court for arbitration. Until the matter was resolved, the residents were disenfranchised, American citizens, but technically residents of no state. Authorities in both Arizona and California agreed to assume no jurisdiction over the disputed area until the matter was resolved.

Most of the inhabitants grew to like this. Instead of being taxed by two states, they were taxed by none. Cars drove around with no license plates. There was no law enforcement. Not long ago, a rancher tippled too heavily one Saturday night in nearby Winterhaven. When he returned to his home in no man's land, he became embroiled in an argument with a neighbor and concluded it by shooting the man to death. Because neither state had jurisdiction over the area, no charges were pressed against the slayer. The victim was buried quietly in Yuma.

This no man's land no longer exists. In 1965 it became a part of the State of Arizona when the federal courts eventually resolved the boundary dispute. Law and taxation finally had come to the last isolated pocket of the old American West.

4

The Ballad of Joaquín Murrieta

On a beach near La Paz, in a cantina near Guadalajara, or on a ranch in New Mexico, wherever the *mariachis* gather, they will sing eventually the ballad of Joaquín Murrieta. In some ways, the ballad parallels the tale of "The Headless Horseman" made famous by Washington Irving. In many parts of the West and Mexico he is a Latin bogeyman and impatient Mexican mothers still hush their querulous children most effectively with the warning that Joaquín Murrieta will get them if they don't watch out.

In California—from Cantua Arroya near Coalinga to Murphy's Diggings in the Mother Lode Country—reports still are made of the sudden appearance of a headless horseman wrapped in a black serape. "I am Joaquín," the apparition wails, "and I want my head." Sometimes the apparition is not seen, but his forlorn cry is heard throughout the passes of the Coast Range where the infamous outlaw roamed.

For years, a head claimed to have been Murrieta's traveled through California immersed in a bottle of brine. It later became a prized attraction in a Barbary Coast saloon in San Francisco. When that city was destroyed by earthquake and fire in 1906, the controversial head disappeared forever. There is strong evidence, however, that the briny head never was attached to the shoulders of the notorious outlaw and that its appearance was part of a carefully planned retirement program for the bloodiest and most ruthless bandit that ever roamed the West.

Billy the Kid, the highly publicized, slope-shouldered,

wide-hipped outlaw of the Southwest killed twenty-one persons before he was slain at the age of twenty-one. Murrieta reigned over California for about three years longer than Billy, and at about the same time, yet the most conservative estimate of the number of his victims is in excess of three hundred. There are some who have glamorized him as the Robin Hood of his time, stealing from the rich and giving to the poor. However, his only charitable impulse that can be documented is an occasion when he spared the life of a robbery victim when he recognized him as a man who had saved his life a few years earlier. His plunder was astronomical, and much of it was shipped into Old Mexico as another contribution to his retirement program.

Joaquín Murrieta came to California from his native Sonora in Mexico about a year before the famous Gold Stampede of 1849. His departure from home was abrupt and designed to escape the wrath of Don José Gonzales who was planning to marry the girl Joaquín loved.

Murrieta lived in the Real de Bayareca between Arispe and Hermosillo, a lush and fertile Sonoran valley. In the same valley lived the beautiful Rosita Carmel Feliz. Both Rosita and Joaquín were educated together in the same convent school, attended the same masses in the old plaza church, and danced together at the fandangos. When she was sixteen and Joaquín eighteen, they fell in love.

In the same valley, lived Don José Gonzales, a gentleman who was very old and very rich. Once prominent in the court of the first Mexican emperor, Augustine Iturbide, his Sonora hacienda was measured by square kilometers instead of acres. He owned five thousand head of blooded horses and more than fifty thousand head of cattle. What Don José wanted, he bought, and when he saw Rosita leaving mass one day, he decided that she should replace the wife he had buried a few months earlier.

Don José opened negotiations with Ramón Feliz, the impoverished father of Rosita. Feliz, apparently envisioning a sharp upturn in his financial status, quickly agreed to the publishing of the banns. However, they were the only persons who agreed to the match. The brother of Rosita, Reyes Feliz, was irate. Equally upset were the two brothers of Joaquín, Claudio and Antonio, as probably would have been an older Murrieta brother, Carlos Jesús, had he not left for somewhere in California a few years earlier.

The day the wedding date was announced, Joaquín and Rosita permanently borrowed two of Don José's blooded horses and in the middle of the night fled from the Real de Bayareca. They were married the following morning in Arispe. They continued their flight along the Camino del Diablo, the deadly and bleak trail that crossed the deserts south of Arizona, and eventually reached the city of Los Angeles.

At this time, Joaquín had two talents. He was an expert horseman. For almost a year, he had worked as a groom in the stables of President López de Santa Anna in Mexico City, and there were no horses in this great stable that Joaquín could not handle. He was also extraordinarily adept in the manipulation of cards. In Los Angeles, he worked at two jobs; a horse trainer and a monte dealer, and in his spare time he roamed through the pueblo looking for his older brother, Carlos Jesús. A few months later, he drifted toward the north with Rosita. He dealt monte in gambling halls at San Juan Bautista and later at San Jose. He opened a store in Stockton, went broke, and then broke horses on a ranch near Mount Diablo. It was here that he learned his brother was in San Francisco.

It was an angry Carlos Jesús that Joaquín found a few weeks later in a gambling hall adjoining the Barbary Coast. Carlos, it seemed, had purchased some land near Hangtown, now known as Placerville, but with the advent of the Gold Rush, the title had somehow become obscured, and the original owner was claiming that the money for the property had never been paid. There was a witness to the transaction, however, a young Mexican named Flores who lived in Hangtown.

Rosita was left at the home of a friend, Manuel Sepulveda, in San Francisco, while the two brothers departed by stage for Sacramento. Horses in the city were scarce, and the price excessive. The Murrietas bought two mules and traveled the rest of the way to Hangtown on the animals. Here they discovered that Flores had moved on to Murphy's Diggings, another day-and-a-half's journey. The town was booming. Gold had been discovered in many adjacent areas, and Murphy's Diggings was the gathering point for all the gamblers, prostitutes, con men, merchants, and miners in all of Calaveras County.

The Murrietas found Flores in a hotel tavern, joined him at a table, and explained the reason for the journey. So far as

Carlos Jesús was concerned, there was nothing secret about his mission. All that he wanted Flores to do was to sign an affidavit prepared by a San Francisco attorney that Flores had been a witness to the payment of the money. It is unknown whether or not Flores signed the papers, but Carlos and Flores did decide to take a look around the town, and Joaquín offered Flores the use of his mule.

A few moments later, Joaquín heard a tremendous uproar in the streets. When he went out to investigate, he discovered his brother and Flores surrounded by some twenty drunken miners. Haranguing Carlos Jesús as a thief was a burly brute, later identified as Bill Lang. It was Lang's contention that the two mules on which Flores and Carlos were riding had been stolen from him and, as mule theft was equally as serious a crime as horse stealing, it took Lang but a few minutes to whip his companions into a hanging mood. Nooses were quickly slipped around the necks of Carlos Jesús and Flores.

Joaquín, crying out in protest, was seized by the gang and escaped hanging by the proverbial hair. As his brother and Flores died above him, Joaquín was bound to the base of the tree. His shirt was ripped from his body. The huge Bill Lang seized a bull whip and lashed it across Joaquín's back thirty-nine times. Each stroke was to leave a permanent scar. Legend says Joaquín did not groan nor writhe once under the torture. Only his eyes seemed to move from one person to another in the gang, lingering on each face to burn it as indelibly on his mind as were the scars on his back. The men commented upon it when they returned to the saloon. Lang was not impressed. "If he comes back to town, we'll hang the sonofabitch," he boasted and poured himself another drink.

Outside, a young gambler named William Wallace Byrnes drifted over to the tree, freed the lacerated Joaquín and cut down the bodies of the two lynching victims. The bodies were draped over Byrnes' horse and taken to the outskirts of the town where Joaquín and the young gambler dug shallow graves and buried the two men. When the brief and silent funeral was over, Brynes took Joaquín to his hotel, where he treated the youth's injured back with soothing ointment. Understandably, this was the start of a long and lasting friendship.

For almost a month, Murrieta remained quietly in Murphy's Diggings despite Lang's threats, savoring his hate for the men who had killed his brother and whetting his appetite on thoughts of the gold that lay in the ground all around him. He staked a small claim in nearby Saw Mill Flat and on it built a small, three-room adobe house with the help of other Mexican miners and his friend Bill Byrnes. When the home was finished, he made a quick trip to San Francisco to pick up Rosita and brought her back to the only home they were to own. And here, if he had been left alone, Joaquín Murrieta probably would have mellowed with age and died, as did most of the other miners, in obscurity. But Joaquín Murrieta was not left alone.

Abutting his claim was a larger one, worked cooperatively by five Americans who were veterans of the recent Mexican-American War. The five Americans bunked together in a large tent, and they made no secret of their hostility to Murrieta and all Mexicans. First, they began to take water from Joaquín's sluice box and, when he objected, they arrogantly began to trench on his claim. The dispute, fanned by racial bias, reached its peak early one evening when the five miners marched into Murrieta's small adobe house. Their spokesman bluntly ordered Joaquín and Rosita to get out and go back to Mexico. The melee started when Joaquín sprang for a bowie knife on the table.

The young Murrieta was no match for his five assailants. Thrown to the floor, he was kicked and pummeled. Rosita, screaming hysterically, snatched up the bowie knife and moved to her husband's aid. She was quickly disarmed and held against the wall by one of the miners. The other four systematically kicked Joaquín into unconsciousness.

Some time later, Bill Byrnes came to the cabin. He first noticed the unconscious Murrieta, ran to a well for a bucket of water, came back and revived his friend. Joaquín staggered into the adjoining room. Spread-eagled and naked on the bed lay Rosita, her limbs bound to the four posts of the cot with the clothes stripped from her body. Her face was battered beyond recognition. As Joaquín moved toward her, Rosita opened her eyes, saw her husband, then sighed deeply. Her eyes closed, and she trembled slightly before she died.

For a long while, Joaquín said nothing. Then slowly he turned from his teen-aged bride and looked toward his companion. His face was as expressionless as a mask. When he spoke, his lips barely moved. "By the blood of Christ, I will kill them all," he said slowly.

The five American miners never went back to their claim. Frontier justice, which would have ignored the beating of Murrieta, would tolerate no such brutal sex crime. Joaquín Murrieta buried his bride near his adobe house and the next day disappeared from Saw Mill Flat.

Several months later, some prospectors crossed a lonely gulch in the Stanislaus River area near Columbia and made a grisly discovery. Lying on the ground were the remains of five bodies. The ears had been sliced from each head. One of the prospectors in the party recognized a ring on the finger of one of the victims. It was identical to a ring worn by a miner he had known in Saw Mill Flat, who had worked the claim next to Murrieta's.

Murrieta, meanwhile, was back in Murphy's Diggings where he opened up a monte game in a local saloon in a partnership with his old friend, Bill Byrnes. He lived with a Yaqui Indian named Joaquín Romero in the nearby village of Los Muertos. If anyone recognized him as the youth who had been lashed so severely some months earlier, they said nothing. By now he spoke fluent English, with no trace of an accent, and was very polite and quite dapper in his dress. Shortly after the monte game was opened, Joaquín Murrieta moved away from the home of his Indian friend to share quarters with two new arrivals in Los Muertos. One of the newcomers was Reyes Feliz, the brother of Rosita. The other was Joaquín's younger brother, Claudio.

One day shortly after the arrival of Claudio, the burly Bill Lang leaned in the door of his saloon watching a miner lead a loaded burro into town. A crowd gathered, and Lang stepped into the street, then caught his breath. Strapped on the back of the small pack animal was a dead man found by the miner in the chaparral along the trail to Angel's Camp. Around the neck of the body was a deep red scar and the ears had been slashed off close to the head. It needed no expert to determine what had happened. The victim had been lassoed, dragged into the brush, and horribly tortured before he died. The sight troubled Bill Lang. The dead man was a friend of his; in fact, one of the twenty who had helped in the hanging of Carlos Jesús Murrieta.

Within the next month, the bodies of four more men were discovered in thickets throughout the hills. All were slain in the same fashion as the first. All had been members of the Murrieta lynching party.

A short time later, a doctor cantered along the trail from Cucumber Gulch to Murphy's Diggings in the late dusk. Hooves drummed behind him on the trail. The doctor turned in his saddle and gasped. A grim figure dressed in black was overtaking him at a tremendous pace. Over the man's head spun a lariat. Suddenly a full moon slid out from behind a cloud, casting its glow over the terrified doctor and the specter. The figure in black reined his mount abruptly and snapped in his lariat. The doctor wheeled, spurred his animal, and raced for Murphy's Diggings although there was no pursuit. The moonlight, which undoubtedly had spared his life, had also given the doctor time to recognize the mysterious murderer as the quiet-speaking monte dealer of Murphy's Diggings.

The motives and real identity of the killer were established shortly after the doctor and a few others of the townspeople called on the startled Bill Byrnes, who luckily was able to convince his guests that he knew nothing of the extracurricular activities of his monte partner. A delegation of heavily-armed miners rode into Los Muertos, but the small house which Joaquín shared with Claudio and Reyes had been abandoned.

The remaining fifteen members of the lynching party sought safety in flight. In pairs and singly, they fled the mining camp. But they could not escape. Joaquin Murrieta toyed with them as would a cat with a crippled bird. The sixth member of the lynching party was slain near Stockton; the seventh, a few days later in far off Knight's Ferry. Murrieta seemed to have an uncanny intelligence system that kept him informed as to the precise whereabouts of his victims.

One potential victim was arrested for a murder in Vallecito and brought to Murphy's Diggings for trial. He escaped, and on the following morning, his earless remains were found on a trail several miles out of town. Another died in a similar fashion in far off Aurora, Nevada. Four were slain on the same day on the banks of the Merced River. Of the twenty men in the group that hung Carlos Jesús Murrieta and Flores, only two escaped the vengeance of Joaquín, and both of these died violently. One was hung before Murrieta could reach him. The other was Bill Lang who was shot down during a brawl.

At twenty-one, Joaquín Murrieta's death toll was three ahead of the total number slain by Billy the Kid.

But many of his fellow Mexicans thought of his vendetta as more than one of a personal nature. Murrieta had been abused by the Americans, but he was not the only Mexican in California to have been maltreated. Many thousands of Mexicans had poured into California during the Gold Rush, still harboring strong anti-American bias engendered during the Mexican War. The Americans resented the Mexican infiltration of the gold fields. The California State Legislature even passed an act which taxed foreign miners exorbitantly, although the tax was repealed a few months later.

Thus, to many Mexicans, in the early stages of his activities, Murrieta was a great hero. For a while he was nicknamed *El Patrio,* The Patriot, and there are some indications that he considered himself a liberator. The name El Patrio, however, did not stick with him long because, as his orgy of terror spread, the North Americans struck back at everything Mexican. Numerous Mexican communities were put to the torch, and all of their inhabitants driven out into the mountains. In one instance an entire Mexican city was leveled by a vengeful mob because Murrieta had hidden within its confines.

The Murrieta band started small, with Joaquín as its chief and Claudio and Reyes Feliz as its two generals. At the beginning, the trio would raid isolated mining camps, slaughter its few inhabitants, then fade back into the hills with stolen gold dust and food. Miners traveling the trails were lassoed from their horses and dragged along the ground until they were dead. Ironically, Joaquín, who was so sensitive to maltreatment of his own race, had an unreasoning hatred toward Orientals. Rare indeed was the Chinese who ever faced Murrieta and walked away alive. He went out of his way to find them, and to him the killing of a Chinese was a sport. More than two hundred of his victims were Orientals.

In its formative period, the gang of bandits ranged over an area bounded on the north by Sutter's Creek and on the south by Jackson and Murphy's Diggings. As its reputation spread, it added to its roster as choice a group of thugs as ever slit a throat. Perhaps the most notorious was a pathological killer named Manuel García, better known as Three-Fingered Jack. Other members of the hard-core center of the horde included Joaquín Valanzuela, a survivor of the notorious Jurata gang of Mexico, Luis Vulvia, Pedro Gonzáles, Juan Senate, and Rafael Escobar. When the band reached its peak in size, each of these men commanded a full company of desperados operating simultaneously over a hundred-mile front. If one of the companies became pressed by a posse it would break apart, only to re-form a few weeks later in a different section of the vast state.

When his revenge for Rosita's death was completed, Joaquín did not brood over his lost love. He went back to Sonora and returned with another childhood sweetheart named Clarita Valero, but he tired of her quickly, sending her back to Sonora. Clarita was replaced briefly by a Dolores García, who in turn was dropped in favor of the beautiful and sophisticated Antonia La Molinera.

There are some tales that Joaquín took La Molinera out of San Jose at dagger point to one of his mountain hideouts. I true, she apparently approved of this manner of courtship. She became his constant companion, sometimes riding the trails with him, dressed like a man; other times his only partner in the fandango houses that Murrieta enjoyed so thoroughly. Except for Bill Byrnes, she was the only person in California who held the complete trust and affection of the bandit.

There were other women in the band, but none with the arrogance, the beauty, and the intelligence of La Molinera. The sweetheart of Pedro Gonzáles was Marquita Vásquez. Less restrictive with their favors were Jesusita Espiosa, a Carmelita and a María Ana Benites. The latter on several occasions was confused with La Molinera, but there never was any doubt as to which was Murrieta's mistress when the two were seen together.

Murrieta surely must have thought himself invincible at the conclusion of his first year of operations. The general public reacted in much the same manner as had the twenty-man mob that lynched Carlos Jesús Murrieta. Whenever the Murrieta horde was rumored to be in the area, townspeople panicked and fled. By the time someone organized a posse, the bandits were gone. Incredible as it may seem, during the first year of operation, the Murrieta band suffered no known casualties, yet the murders attributed to the band were in excess of one hundred and fifty.

Many of the killings were wanton. A newspaper, the Alta *Californian*, reported an incident where Murrieta rode into San Andreas, singled out three North Americans on the Main Street, and shot them dead. "On Thursday," the paper reported, "Joaquín rode through San Andreas and shot three Americans as he passed through the street. Joaquín is a young man and must be one of the best shots with a revolver in this or any other country as all three men were shot through the neck." The newspaper did not bother to mention the names of the victims.

As the horde grew larger and bolder, towns posted armed guards around their communities. Stagecoaches refused to operate unless accompanied by heavily armed patrols. Miners abandoned their claims. The citizens of many communities in the Mother Lode Country banded together themselves to form a small army that had but one objective—to trap and hang Murrieta.

The bandit gang, in view of this threat, split apart temporarily, but this time the strategy was not completely successful. Two of the gang were trapped in Sonora, near Marysville, and shot to death after they wounded a deputy sheriff. Another was hung in Mokelume Hill and still another in Angel's Camp. Murrieta apparently regarded these casualties as a matter of lese majesty. He called the band together again and struck out at everything. Oddly, most of his rage was directed toward the Chinese mining camps. He burned down a saw mill, killing three men too old to join the army, then, believing the army to be much farther south, attempted a retaliatory raid on Mokelume Hill. He nearly was ambushed at Chaparral Hill as he moved toward the town, losing a half dozen of his gang.

The citizens' army trailed Murrieta to a mountain community named Yaqui, composed primarily of Mexicans. This posse was well over one hundred men, all of them angry and bitter. When they could not find any sign of the bandit or his followers in the community, and when no one would tell them where they had gone, the army destroyed the town. Systematically, it put the torch to every home, every store, and every building in Yaqui. Every inhabitant was driven homeless into the hills. Today there are no signs of Yaqui. Even its location is a matter of disagreement among the oldtimers of the Mother Lode Country. Upon its return to San Andreas, the posse, still in the mood for destruction, burned out the entire Mexican section of the city, sending hundreds of Mexicans destitute into the hills.

Although cruel, the destruction of these two communities acquired the desired result. The Mexicans now feared the citizens' army more than it feared the wrath of Murrieta. No longer did they think of him as El Patrio because he had become responsible for their own misfortune, and thus, no longer did they hide and feed members of the gang in their homes. It no longer became a status symbol for a Mexican youth to ride with Murrieta. The size of the band dwindled rapidly, and Murrieta decided to turn his attention elsewhere temporarily. He chose the city of San Jose as his headquarters, a large city many miles to the east in the fertile Santa Clara Valley.

Inside the city, the gang lived quietly, but the harassment of ranchers and travelers outside of the city reached such proportions that it soon was known to all that the bandit, Murrieta, was in the area.

The reaction was as expected. Deputy Sheriff Robert Clark formed a posse of the city's more stalwart citizens and eventually trapped two members of the band near the foothills of the Santa Cruz Mountains. The two captives were brought into San Jose for trial. Among the spectators at the proceedings where the two bandits were sentenced to be hung was Murrieta, his identity apparently known only to the defendants.

The day after the two bandits were executed Deputy Sheriff Robert Clark was tipped anonymously that still another bandit of Murrieta's would be at a fandango dance that night in the San Jose Plaza. As Clark leaned against the wall, listening to the music and watching for his man, a woman suddenly screamed. The music stopped, and the dancers parted to disclose a youthful and handsome Mexican waving a knife in front of a terrified girl whom he had pinned against the wall.

Clark reacted as would any deputy. He disarmed the irate Mexican youth easily and bustled him off to a justice of the peace who was holding night court for just such occasions.

Clark's captive was friendly and understanding, enough so that the deputy suggested to the court that he be assessed only a small fine of $12. The court agreed.

"I don't have that much money with me," the defendant said apologetically, "but if the Sheriff will be kind enough to walk with me to my home I will give him the money there."

Both the court and Clark were agreeable to this suggestion from such a pleasant and inoffensive young man. They left the building and strolled along the dark and narrow streets toward the Santa Clara Mission.

"Incidentally, I have a surprise for you," the Mexican said presently.

The deputy paused and smiled toward his companion.

"I am Joaquín Murrieta," the man said in the same cavalier manner, "and I have brought you here to kill you."

The dying Clark's body was found a short time later, a hand on the butt of his revolver.

The gang moved back toward the east. From Stockton, the river flows down to San Francisco Bay, navigable even today for ocean-going vessels. At this time, it was the more popular and, with bandits like Murrieta roaming the countryside, the safest way to travel to San Francisco.

A few days after Clark died in San Jose, a two-masted schooner cast off from the Stockton Wharf. On board were three sailors and two miners with approximately $30,000 worth of gold dust. The river writhed through the land on the first part of its journey to the bay, little more than a slough at that time with tall bulrushes lining the river bank.

It is unlikely that any on board noticed the small rowboat that glided out from the thick brush along the bank and, like a leech, fastened itself on the side of the schooner. Moments later, four men leaped on the deck. The helmsman was shot instantly. One sailor smashed the skull of one of the bandits with a belaying pin but he died a moment later when a bullet struck him in the head. Within a few seconds the miners were slain as was the remaining sailor. Murrieta, Three-Fingered Jack, and Valanzuela slipped back into the stolen rowboat and paddled away with the loot.

When word of the murders reached Stockton, the touch of Murrieta was suspected. A five-thousand-dollar reward was posted for his capture and a twenty-five-man posse was formed to track down the outlaw. The posse was no match for the wily Murrieta who, on about the fourth day of the chase, ambushed it, killing twenty-four of its members. The only man to survive was a Jim Boyce who, ironically, was the only member who had ever seen Murrieta. The slaughter of the posse increased Murrieta's unpopularity markedly. There was talk in Stockton of building a 250-man permanent posse to run him down. The Mother Lode Country was still un-friendly, and San Jose was most inhospitable. Once again, the gang was disbanded and told to drift down to Los Angeles where a rendezvous would be held in nearby San Gabriel.

Murrieta, Ramón Feliz, Three-Fingered Jack, and Valan-

zuela traveled to the City of the Angels with María Ana
Benites, Mariquita Vásquez, Carmelita, and another girl. La
Molinera was sent on ahead. It was planned as a nice vaca-
tion trip. The only business conducted occurred at Tejon
Pass where Murrieta noticed a particularly fine horse and
decided to take it along with him.

It was a mistake. The horse belonged to a close friend of
Chief Zapatero of the Tejons, and he had no intention of
letting the animal become the property of a few transients.
The night after the horse had been stolen, a band of Tejons
surrounded the sleeping Murrieta party, disarmed them, and
marched them some fifteen miles to a stockade in Zapatero's
village. A few Indian braves had accomplished easily what a
dozen armed posses had been unable to do in the north. The
Murrieta party was kept in the stockade for a couple of
weeks, then stripped of their finery, valuables, and horses,
marched to the edge of the Tejon domain, and turned loose.
The terrorist outlaw and his companions skulked across the
county by night until, on the outskirts of Los Angeles, they
reached the home of a hoodlum friend known as Mountain
Jim Wilson. Here horses, pistols, and clothes were found in
the usual manner, and the Murrieta group was able to regain
some of its usual arrogance.

About a week later, Pedro Gonzáles and Juan Cardoza
drifted into San Buenaventura in their trek to the southland.
In this seacoast town south of Santa Barbara was a Los Angeles deputy sheriff named Harry Love. A former Texas
ranger, Love came to California in the Gold Rush, went
broke, and became a deputy at Santa Barbara before taking
a similar position in Los Angeles. A tough-speaking, ugly, and
profane man, Love was quick to jump to conclusions. Earlier,
a horse had been stolen from J. A. Carver, and the thief later
had shot a tavern keeper. In San Buenaventura, Love was told
that Cardoza, well known as a horse thief, had headed south
a couple of hours earlier. Love knew Cardoza, but not
Gonzáles.

At a tavern, a few miles south, Love spotted the horses of
the two men and he paused outside to wait for them to
emerge. Cardoza came out first and, seeing Love, bounded
around the corner of the building and jumped on his horse.
Gonzáles rushed out at the sound of the shooting and was
immediately taken prisoner. Love tethered Gonzáles to the
saddle of his horse and set out for Los Angeles, Gonzáles

trailing behind. Cardoza, meanwhile, rode at breakneck speed to San Gabriel where Murrieta was waiting. The deputy and his prisoner traveled all night, but the pace necessarily was slow. At dawn, in the Conejo Valley north of Los Angeles, Murrieta overtook Love and Gonzáles. Love was faced with a difficult decision. He was outnumbered by the bandits and he could not fight them. He could not escape while towing a captive, yet after all this work he did not want to lose his prisoner. The answer that occurred to Love was reasonable. Turning in his saddle, he shot Gonzáles, cut him loose, kicked the stolen horse free, then rode for his life to Los Angeles. Thus, Gonzáles became the first in the top command of the Murrieta gang to die.

Possibly the death of Gonzáles was an omen. Murrieta found it much more difficult to operate around Los Angeles. He lived in San Gabriel with La Molinera, María Benites, Reyes, and Carmelita, but for some reason the band could not get organized as it had in the north. Part of the trouble Murrieta blamed upon the vigilantes who were prone to shoot as unpredictably as any bandit. Two members of his band were shot down for no reason at all.

A deputy sheriff from Santa Barbara, Robert Wilson, heard of the $5,000 reward for Murrieta and learned also that the notorious bandit was hiding somewhere in Los Angeles. He rode south and when in the city, he spread the word as to the reason for his visit.

One morning he heard a fracas in front of the Bella Union Hotel where he was staying and strolled outside. Two men were flailing away at each other, neither one doing much damage. A few dozen peons in sombreros watched the fight curiously. Another Mexican, slouched in his saddle, came down the street, and when he drew abreast of Wilson, he casually reined in his horse. "I hear you are looking for me," he said casually.

Wilson looked up. "Who in the hell are you?"

"Joaquín Murrieta."

Wilson reached for his gun, but he was not fast enough. He died, a bullet in his brain, with his gun half out of his holster.

This was the type of murder that excited the vigilantes. In the ensuing sweep, three members of the Murrieta band were snared and hung. Murrita reacted in the same manner as he had in Angel's Camp.

One of the most prominent members of the vigilantes in Los Angeles was General Joshua H. Bean, a former mayor of San Diego and a major general in the state militia. On the night of November 21, 1852, General Bean was assassinated by Murrieta in San Gabriel as he was returning to his quarters in the old mission building.

The reaction to this murder was greater than anything Murrieta had ever experienced. The vigilantes swarmed like locusts over San Gabriel. Murrieta and Three-Fingered Jack escaped into the hills. Caught by the vigilantes, however, were María Benites and Reyes Feliz, along with numerous others of his followers.

There was a trial. María Benites testified that a cobbler named Cipriano Sandoval had killed the general. Reyes Feliz was taken to Los Angeles for a citizens' trial where it was discovered that he was the brother-in-law of the notorious Murrieta and a member of his gang. Also caught in San Gabriel was Benito López, another member of Murrieta's band.

The trial did not last long. The Sunday after the death of General Bean, Reyes Feliz, Benito López and the poor cobbler, Cipriano Sandoval, were hanged along with another murderer at Fort Hill in downtown Los Angeles to the cheers of a crowd of several hundred men and women who gathered to witness the executions. Two of the top command were gone.

The bandit, with Three-Fingered Jack and two others, retreated farther from the city, to hide out in Mariposa. Word was sent out for the band to rendezvous at Mariposa. Luis Vulvia, Juan Senate, and four other members of the gang headed for the rendezvous, but on their way out of the city they paused to rob and kill a wealthy French merchant. A squad of deputies headed by City Marshal Jack Whaling intercepted the bandits midway between Los Angeles and San Gabriel. The bandits escaped after killing Whaling, but almost at once the identity of the killers was known, and they were identified as henchmen of Murrieta. Rewards of $1500 were posted for Vulvia or Senate, dead or alive.

The following morning, a bull cart driven by a small boy and accompanied by a well-dressed Mexican horseman pulled up in front of the Los Angeles jail. The horseman called for the Sheriff and jailer to come out. He was, the horseman explained, Atanacio Moreno, formerly of Yaqui. The preceding day, he continued, he had been kidnaped by five men, and as he was being taken along the highway, he overpowered and slew the lot. Two of the men were identified as Vulvia and Senate. The other three were unknown.

Moreno was an overnight hero with his five corpses. He collected the reward, but his hours of glory did not last long. When he tried to sell some of the merchandise stolen from the murdered Frenchman to a local pawnbroker, he was arrested. Word was passed to the proper authorities that he had been a close companion of Senate and Vulvia in many of the city's dives. When questioned about this, Moreno admitted that he had indeed been a member of the Murrieta band but that he had received a message from God to mend his ways and that he had interpreted this as a heavenly directive to do away with his evil comrades. Apparently the courts accepted this explanation as a reasonable one. He was tried only for the theft of the Frenchman's valuable, found guilty, and sentenced to four years in prison. Upon his release, he disappeared and presumably returned to Mexico.

On the same day that Moreno was found guilty of his minor offense, Mountain Jim and Valanzuela were trapped by sheriff's deputies in a San Diego tavern. Valanzuela shot his way out, but Mountain Jim was captured and within a period of a half hour, was tried, found guilty, and hung. Valanzuela successfully worked his way back to Los Angeles, puzzled as to how the posse had traced him to that particular tavern in San Diego. Both he and Mountain Jim were completely unknown in that border city. The only reason for his being in the tavern was to pick up possible orders from Murrieta.

In Los Angeles, Valanzuela went to the brothel where Carmelita was employed temporarily, and it was from her that he learned of the perfidity of María Benites. In return for her information, the authorities had gratefully released her from custody. Carmelita had no idea where she had gone, but Valanzuela had solved the mystery as to how he had been trapped in San Diego. From Carmelita, he also learned the whereabouts of Murrieta.

A short time later, Valanzuela appeared at Joaquín's hideout in Mariposa where he solved the other mystery as to what had happened to María Benites. She was bedding with the notorious bandit while he waited for his scattered band to reach Mariposa. It would be hard to guess who was the most surprised, Valanzuela, by finding her there, María, by seeing

Valanzuela alive, or Murrieta, when he learned that his current mistress was surely a sheriff's agent. The bandit, however, was no gallant, nor was he inclined to give his mistress the benefit of the doubt. He ordered Three-Fingered Jack to saddle up the horses, then casually emptied the contents of his revolver, six shots, into the body of his voluptuous paramour. As she lay moaning on the floor, he sprinkled kerosene around the adobe house and then, as he departed, tossed a match into it. Incredibly, María Benites survived and years later, in San Jose, where she settled, delighted in shucking her clothes to display the half-dozen healed bullet holes left by Murrieta's bullets.

The bandit chief picked up the remnants of his horde and, skirting the coast, worked his way north. A rancher was murdered near Santa Barbara. Another ranch was raided near San Luis Obispo with three more victims. Rumors began to circulate from one end of the state to the other that Murrieta was recruiting the largest band of his career, and citizens from San Francisco to Los Angeles prepared for another seige of terror.

Governor John Bigler added a $1,000 reward for Murrieta, dead or alive, to the other many rewards posted. The State Assembly convened at Benecia and accepted a proposal from Harry Love in southern California that he form a private company to hunt down the elusive outlaw. The solons gave him ninety days to complete the task, limited the size of the group to twenty men, and gave it the name of the California Rangers. It was at this point that the saga of Joaquín Murrieta took its most bizarre twist.

The recruiting for the rangers took place in northern California and among the early volunteers was a young man named William Wallace Byrnes. At first, the dour Harry Love was unimpressed.

"But I am one of the few men in California who can recognize him," Byrnes said. "If you're going after Murrieta, you must have someone along who can recognize him when you catch up to him."

Harry Love finally conceded that Byrnes would indeed be an asset. Thus, when the California Rangers took to the road a week later, one member of the company was the best friend Murrieta ever had.

The outlaw was reported to be in San Jose when the rangers started their campaign in June of 1853. He was staying at the ranch of Joaquín Guerra on the outskirts of the city where he murdered the proprietor of a saloon whom Murrieta thought might have recognized him. A short time later, he killed an Indian on the Guerra Ranch whom he feared might betray him. The Indian thus enjoyed the unique distinction of being the last man known to have been murdered by the notorious outlaw.

Oddly, the chase by Harry Love's California Rangers, and Murrieta's flight, was a slow-motion affair. The rangers arrived in Santa Clara County and leisurely set up camp the day after Murrieta, with an estimated twenty men, drifted away from the Guerra ranch. Newspapers in both San Francisco and Los Angeles reported the progress of both companies, one commenting that the bandit appeared to be "remarkably docile" on this trip. Murrieta, although still traveling slowly, outdistanced the much slower-moving rangers and, by the time the bandit reached San Luis Obispo, the rangers were still sweeping the foothills of the Santa Cruz Mountains many miles to the north.

The California *Police Gazette* reported laconically that, while passing through San Luis Obispo, Murrieta was seen conversing with an aristocratic woman of Mexican appearance. The woman was traveling by coach and, after the tryst, continued to the north. The bandit continued toward the south, and the farther he traveled, the smaller dwindled his band. A posse in Santa Barbara reported it had chased the elusive outlaw to the Santa Monica Mountains outside of Los Angeles before it lost him. He was next reported to have camped in the mountains southeast of San Juan Capistrano.

Meanwhile, the California Rangers were camped at San Juan Bautista at least four hundred miles to the north. It was here that Bill Byrnes proved his value to the rangers. He brought into camp a young, darkly beautiful woman and took her straight to Captain Harry Love.

The woman had a most interesting story for the commander of the California Rangers. Her name, she said, was Antonia La Molinera, and for a long time she had been the mistress of Joaquín Murrieta. But she had become tired of the bandit and had fled to Los Angeles with Pancho Daniels to start a new life. Murrieta, she continued, had sworn to kill her and he surely would succeed. Her only hope for happiness lay in the death of Murrieta, and thus she was prepared to betray him. He was at that moment, she said, hiding in the Cantua Arroya, about two days distant to the southeast.

Bill Brynes gravely nodded his head. La Molinera's information undoubtedly was correct. To Harry Love, her information appeared authentic, and as Bill Byrnes gallantly escorted La Molinera back to the town, Love made preparations for the showdown.

The rangers left San Juan Bautista at dawn and rode hard all day. By late the following afternoon they were on the east side of the Coast Range and by night, they were within sight of the narrow defile which led into Cantua Arroya. At dawn the following morning, the rangers cautiously moved into the canyon. Around a turn, they saw the smoke of a campfire rising straight into still air from a mesa a short distance above them.

There were seven Mexicans in the camp when the rangers galloped in. One was frying bacon over the fire. Five others were watching the cook sleepily, and the seventh was washing down the legs of his horse. The last ranger to come up over the lip of the mesa was Bill Byrnes. He reined his mount, then suddenly pointed his finger at the Mexican by the horse. "It's Joaquín!" he cried.

The rangers immediately opened fire. The slender man by the horse leaped on the animal's back and, using it as a shield, raced out of the camp. One of the rangers, William T. Henderson, went after the fleeing youth. The remainder fought point blank with the others around the campfire and, when four of the Mexicans were killed, accepted the other two as prisoners. None of the rangers were hurt.

Henderson caught up with his quarry some two miles further up the canyon, first bringing down the horse and then the man. When the battle was over, the rangers were faced with a problem. The rewards for Murrieta's capture were large, but it would be a struggle to carry his body back to civilization. It was Bill Byrnes who solved the problem. "Hell, it ain't much work to pack back the head," he said, and with a hatchet and a bowie knife he severed the head of Henderson's victim and tied it to his saddle pommel. The hand of one of the victims at the campfire site, reportedly with one finger missing, also was whacked off. The rest of the bodies were left where they had fallen, as, with head and hand and two prisoners, the rangers started back. By the time they reached the first town, however, one of their prisoners was gone. Antonio López, Love reported, had committed suicide by jumping into a mountain creek. The remaining prisoner, a sullen man who refused to open his mouth, made it as far as Martinez before he was taken by a mob from the rangers' custody and strung up to a nearby tree.

The California legislature was most grateful. In addition to the reward posted by Governor Bigler and numerous other rewards posted by communities from Stockton to Los Angeles, the legislature voted an additional $5,000 bonus to the intrepid Harry Love. Henderson's share of the reward money was augmented by a tour of the state in which the citizens, for a one dollar fee, could see the head, the hand, and the man who killed Murrieta. Later, the head was sold at an auction for $35 and eventually wound up in the Barbary Coast saloon where it remained on display until it was destroyed in the disastrous earthquake and fire of 1906. No one seriously questioned its authenticity. Love was a hero and the deeds of heroes are not questioned until they have lost their following.

The first serious doubts were raised by a San Francisco newspaperman, R. M. Daggett. Several years after the fight in Cantua Arroya, Daggett traced Byrnes to Fresno, California, and interviewed him on the anniversary of Murrieta's death.

"One pickled head is as good as any other if no one knows the difference," Byrnes told Daggett. "Joaquín will have to be killed once more to entitle him to a burial."

It is a most interesting statement inasmuch as it was Byrnes who rode into the camp of the outlaw and started the chase that led to Murrieta's death . . . or someone else's death. There are some who claim that Murrieta lived to be an old man back in his native state of Sonora. Among these was an aging Catholic priest in Santa Barbara who had married Antonio Murrieta to his bride in Los Angeles. After reading of the death of Bill Byrnes several years later, he told a newspaper friend that Joaquín was still alive, living in Magdalena, Sonora, Mexico, and that he had been given this information by Antonio.

Love died after being shot in the aftermath of a domestic squabble. All of the other members of his posse, except Byrnes, died violently. La Molinera disappeared, and this too is in the tale sung to a guitar.

There are some who claim that there never was a Joaquín Murrieta, but this is a most difficult theory to accept. There are far too many records attesting to his existence, and newspapers of that era carried too many stories of the fearsome Mexican bandit "who plunders the entire state with impunity."

Whether Murrieta died a young man in the foothills of the Sierra Nevada or an old man in the foothills of the Sierra Madre, his name will remain in the legends of the mysterious west for many years to come. Weekend explorers still comb the hills in the Mother Lode Country looking for the vast amounts of treasure that Murrieta is believed to have buried.

5

The Explanation of Peg Leg's Black Gold

Around the Caribbean, the search for sunken treasure aboard lost Spanish galleons has been going on for years. In recent times, with the advent of scuba diving, more and more of these valuable wrecks have been discovered. In the West, the hunt has been for lost treasure, either in mines, caves, or missions, and the modern devices used here are the electronic metal detectors, the four-wheel-drive jeep and the sand-dune buggy. Yet the percentage of successes among the western treasure seeker has been much lower than his Caribbean counterpart. There have been recurrent tales of findings from Texas to Arizona, but usually the treasure to be harvested comes from the gullible who buy stock in companies formed by the finders. One of the most notable exceptions concerns the elusive black gold of Peg Leg Smith lost well over a century ago in the arid desert area of southern California. For years it has been the target of prospectors. The search for the Lost Peg Leg Mine is the basis for a society that meets annually in Borrego Springs, California, and some hopefuls have spent most of their lives searching in vain for this mine.

Very recently, however, evidence has been advanced that indicates that the lost treasure of Peg Leg Smith not only has been located and harvested, but also that it was not his and it never was a mine.

Peg Leg undoubtedly was one of the most ubiquitous one-legged characters ever to stump the West. Peglegophiles disagree on almost every aspect of his life, from his place of birth to his place of death. He was born either in Boston, Chicago, or Kentucky. He died in a San Diego saloon brawl, or in the arms of a sympathetic French physician named De Corse in San Bernardino, or as a broken and discredited old man in San Francisco County Hospital in 1866. There is no disagreement, however, upon the fact that Peg Leg stumbled upon an area in southern California where black gold nuggets were strewn with the profusion of hailstones after a late spring squall. Nor is there any disagreement to the contention that Peg Leg was a most irascible rustler and foul-tempered drunk.

There is a story told, tongue-in-cheek, by native Nevadans over one of Peg Leg's adventures that may provide a clue as to the source of Peg Leg's black gold. Teaming up with a group of Ute Indians, Peg Leg, in the mid 1830s, undertook one of the most spectacular rustling raids in the history of the frontier country.

With his Ute friends, Peg Leg swooped through scores of southern California corrals in a night-long foray and by morning the band was driving more than three thousand head of blooded horses through Cajon Pass toward the high desert country to the east. Understandably upset, the victims of the raids saddled the few mounts left by the rustlers and took off in pursuit. Twice they came within shooting range of Peg Leg and his Utes; once at Bitter Springs, another time at Resting Springs. On both occasions the rustlers escaped under cover of darkness. Eventually Peg Leg and his band came to a small oasis where the stolen horses were watered, then driven into nearby barren foothills.

Shortly before nightfall the posse galloped into the oasis where it was decided to camp briefly before pushing after the quarry. When all were bedded down and the horses corraled on the edge of the oasis, Peg Leg and his Indian friends slithered into the camp and added the mounts of the posse to the herd rustled a couple of days earlier.

The hapless pursuers were forced to hike more than two hundred miles back to their homes and thus, say Nevadans, won the unique distinction of being the first Californians to go home broke from Las Vegas, as the oasis later was to be known.

Peg Leg's interest in horse trade is well authenticated by the records of the Spanish dons which attest to the losses suffered from the raids of the one-legged renegade and his

Indian followers. Rewards were posted, but Peg Leg held the luck of Zorro and never was captured. Thus, in view of his highly successful record as a horse thief, it is difficult to believe the story as to how he discovered his black gold, yet oddly, this part of the legend generally is accepted by Peglegophiles.

According to the legend, Peg Leg turned his attention away from horse rustling in favor of trapping. He formed a partnership with two men named Maurice Le Duc and Ewing Young, and during the spring, the three men were unusually successful in acquiring a large number of fur pelts in the mountain areas of Utah and New Mexico. The legend continues that Young, the leader of the group, sent Peg Leg and Le Duc to the nearest market with the pelts. If this is true, then Young must be considered a most naive frontiersman, to entrust his share of the furs to a man with the reputation of Peg Leg Smith. The nearest market place was Santa Fe, yet Peg Leg and Le Duc struck out with their furs for the distant Spanish settlements of Los Angeles and San Diego.

It is here that the legend veers to the more usual pattern. The two men, riding mules and leading their fur-laden pack train, drove directly into one of the most dangerous and treacherous sections of the United States, that incredibly hot desert area, in some spots more than two hundred feet below sea level, where heat can dehydrate a man within a few hours. Even today, in some areas, stranded motorists have collapsed and died within a few hundred yards of their stalled vehicles while hiking for aid. Savage sandstorms can force a man to his knees, and never will he rise again.

Yet the legend has Peg Leg, his companion, and his pack train wandering for three days in such a storm with their water supply exhausted. When the winds eventually died, Peg Leg searched immediately for a high spot of ground where he could go to obtain his bearings. In the distance and in the fading light of day, he saw three low hills or buttes. He rode quickly to the tallest of these and climbed it. Beyond the buttes lay more desert and beyond the desert were mountains where he knew he could find fresh spring water. On his way back down the butte, the legend continues, he noticed some black stones lying on the slope. He dismounted, picked up a couple of handfuls which he placed in his pocket, then rode back to his waiting partner.

The storm had killed several of his pack animals, and the

pelts they carried were, by necessity, cached. The two men struck out for the distant mountain, reaching it in the night. Here they found water and rested. A few days later they arrived in San Diego and disposed of the furs they carried with them. Several versions of the legend say that Peg Leg and Le Duc returned to their cache and brought back the rest of the pelts. Other versions make no mention of this, and none relate Ewing Young's reaction over the failure of his partners to return with his share of the profits.

At this point the legend splinters. One version has Peg Leg discovering that his little black rocks, picked up on the slope of the butte, were in reality almost pure gold nuggets. Another version attributes the discovery to the good French doctor in San Bernardino. Still another gives credit to an innkeeper in San Diego who kept one of the rocks after he threw Peg Leg out of his hostelry because of his foul talk and boisterous manner. There is little doubt but that Peg Leg did carry a pocketful of black nuggets and that he launched a treasure hunt that has lasted well over a century. Prospectors and desert rats discussed the possible location of the Peg Leg Mine, and thousands of theories were advanced as to its location. In recent years the legend of Peg Leg's black gold was being accepted slowly as little more than a myth. As southern California's population swelled into the millions it spilled into the desert areas. Desert resorts, such as Palm Springs and Palm Desert, brought in more people, as did irrigation for the huge gardens of the Imperial Valley. The desert swarmed with weekend rock hounds who scoured the ground to the very edge of the treacherous sand sea in which Peg Leg allegedly almost foundered. No one ever saw the three buttes of the legend. No one ever found any black gold . . . not until March of 1955, and the mysterious "New Peg Leg" who did find it kept his secret for a decade.

For years, *Desert* magazine, which is published in Palm Desert, had regularly received letters from old and young prospectors advancing theories as to the location of the lost mine. The old timers finally "had figgered out" where the gold was located. Some wanted a grub stake from the magazine to "go git it." Others wanted advice.

In March of 1965, a package arrived at the offices of the publication. In the package were two large black nuggets of gold and a letter that was unsigned. Its writer claimed he had found the lost Peg Leg gold and offered the nuggets as proof.

"Perhaps it is time to give hope to those hardy souls who have spent months and years of their lives searching for lost bonanzas," the anonymous writer said. "There have always been doubting Thomases who claimed that lost mines and treasures of the desert were nothing but figments of somebody's imagination. Well, now it is time to prove that at least one lost desert bonanza has been discovered—and not lost again, for I know exactly where it is."

The New Peg Leg has delighted in passing out hints in both the original and subsequent letters, each accompanied by another black gold nugget, as to the location of the treasure. It is on top of a small hill at the head of a wash within thirty miles of the Salton Sea. He is a rock hound, not a treasure seeker nor prospector. Within the past decade, he has picked up from the ground more than $300,000 worth of nuggets and he doubts if there are many more left. He has disposed of these mostly in Alaska and Canada and he goes into considerable detail as to the methods he used to remove the black oxidization on the nuggets that, even in Canada and Alaska, might trigger someone's memory of the lost Peg Leg gold.

Perhaps the most significant statement made by the mysterious rock hound is that in which he says most of the nuggets were lying loose on the ground. When he returned to the area with a metal detector, more nuggets were found in depths ranging from four inches to two feet, and all within a comparatively small area of approximately sixty yards encompassing the side of the slope and a small mound.

The nuggets accompanying subsequent letters sent to the magazine were analyzed and the results concurred with those stated by the elusive New Peg Leg. Each contained about 70 per cent gold, 20 per cent silver and 10 per cent copper, the latter causing the oxidation which gave the nuggets their black color.

When this was printed in the magazine, it sounded a familiar note to California historian Robert Buck. He knew that almost all of the gold ever mined in California contained 10 to 20 per cent silver alloy from the days of its most publicized discovery at Sutter's Creek. With one exception, none contained copper.

Several years prior to the California Gold Rush that started with the Sutter's Creek discovery, gold was being mined quietly in northern California. The mines were owned by the wealthy and aristocratic Peralta family of Sonora, Mexico, and were located in Calaveras County. It was black gold and the alloys were about 20 per cent silver and 10 per cent copper. The operation of the mines was overseen by two of the Peralta sons.

The Peraltas made no attempt to process the nuggets in California, preferring to send gold in its natural disguise by pack train over the long overland route to Sonora which went through the central part of California, east of Los Angeles, then south along the eastern side of the mountains, then across the desert near what later became the boundary of Mexico and the United States when California became a part of the latter nation.

The historian recalled another incident recorded in old archives of Mexican California. In the early 1830s a large pack train carrying ore from the peralta mine set out on its long journey to Sonora. One of the Peralta sons was to accompany the pack train but, feeling the urge for relaxation and entertainment, he sent the slow-moving caravan on ahead and detoured through San Francisco where he dallied for three days.

He was unable to catch up with the pack train. When he arrived in Sonora, the caravan of ore-laden horses had not arrived, and for a while it was thought that he had somehow passed them en route. The pack train never did arrive in Sonora. It had vanished.

It is the historian's theory, and one in which the mysterious New Peg Leg concurs, that the pack train was ambushed by Indians who sought only the horses. After slaying the pack train attendants, the Indians cut loose the senseless load the pack animals carried and disappeared with the horses. Thus, this theory continues, the black gold found so easily on the ground is that which was carried by the lost Peralta caravan.

Add to this another theory. Peg Leg Smith was a known bandit, a horse thief and a semi-illiterate drunk who, about the same time the Peralta caravan was passing through southern California, was raiding the *estancias* of the dons with the aid of his Ute Indian band of some 150 braves. The horses in the caravan would appear an easy target. The load they carried would have puzzled Peg Leg more than his followers, and it would have made sense for him to have pocketed a few of the peculiar rocks to see why they were worth packing. He had no mining experience. And, when he discovered that he had lost a fortune for the want of some horses, it might explain why he became such an irascible lush. He would have taken no bearings on the scene of an ambush.

It is just a theory, but it seems more logical than the account in the legend that he lived three days without water in a raging desert sandstorm, that when parched with thirst, he paused to pick up stones and that he had given up horse rustling for a few months to go fur trapping in Utah.

The New Peg Leg mentioned in one letter that he had discovered an old Spanish silver belt buckle at the site of the black gold. It would be interesting to know if he also noticed a stray tibia or so when he was harvesting the lost Peg Leg gold . . . or the lost Peralta gold.

The ubiquitous Peg Leg has been so closely associated with his lost black gold that many have overlooked the significance of the one-legged rustler's favorite horse, a beast named either Bounty or Mounty. It was a peculiar animal and possibly it was the only living thing for which Peg Leg had a genuine affection. There were perhaps half a dozen similar horses in the band of Ute Indians that Peg Leg led on his forays. These horses were fur coated like a buffalo and had the short back and powerful shoulders of an Arabian stallion. They could easily outrun the fastest horses of a pursuing posse, yet they were as durable as any mustangs on the western range.

One of the more common misconceptions in history is that the horse was introduced to the New World by Hernan Cortes, the first of the conquistadores to invade Central America. Possibly they were the first such animals seen by the Indians on the eastern coast of Mexico, but the horse was well known in the western part of the hemisphere. On the desert floor near what is now Blythe, California, there are, even today, huge intaglios, up to 170 feet long, of men, women, and horses that slow-forming desert varnish indicates were laid out many years before the arrival of the Spaniards. These were discovered, incidentally, by Air Force pilots on desert maneuvers during World War II. Fossil bones of tiny horses have been found around the area of the mysterious cliff dwellers in New Mexico. Stories still persist that herds of tiny horses roam in the remote reaches of the Grand Canyon. These tiny horses do exist, not ponies, but full-grown horses weighing under fifty pounds. The Regina Winery in Etiwanda, California, has a half dozen, imported from Argentina at a cost of $5,000 each, but the only evidence ever found as to their existence in the Grand Canyon is a mysterious picture of one wrapped around the shoulders of an unidentified man. Quite probably this is a fake photo as the writers can find no record of any person who actually has seen one of the diminutive horses that allegedly roam in the Grand Canyon.

It is a different story, however, with the fur-coated horses used by Peg Leg and some of his Ute Indians. They are being bred today on the large Three Bar Ranch in central Nevada, and they provide another link in the chain of evidence that the West was well traveled long before Christopher Columbus set off on his highly publicized voyage.

The ranch was founded by Peter Damele in 1898. While on a horse-hunting expedition in the nearby Pete Hanson Mountain Range, Damele and his cowhands came upon an exceptionally large herd of wild horses and successfully drove them into a corral constructed at the bottom of a large canyon. In the herd were three horses of a type that Damele had never seen. They had shaggy fur coats, almost identical to the coat of a buffalo. He found them much more intelligent and easier to train than the average mustang.

A blooded horse can outrun any mustang over a short course, but it lacks the durability of the mustang. Damele discovered that these strange animals with the peculiar curly coat had more than twice the stamina of the mustang. In the ensuing months, he made another discovery. The fur-coated horses readily bred with the mustangs and theirs was the dominant strain. It made no difference if a fur-coated stallion serviced a mustang mare nor if a fur-coated mare was bred to a mustang; the foal invariably had all the characteristics of the strange breed. He deduced that the curly-haired horses had joined the wild herd shortly before it was trapped.

When Damele died, his son Peter Damele, Jr., took over the operation of the Three Bar Ranch. Shortly thereafter, and in some manner now forgotten, he learned that his mysterious curly haired horses were similar to fur coated steeds common to Mongolia. Quietly, Damele began an investigation that was to last several years, including a lengthy correspondence with the Soviet Department of Agriculture. The breed still was common in both Mongolia and Russia. The breed was known to the Russians as the Bashkir, the name coming from the state on the east slope of the Ural Mountains. It had been used for centuries by the hardy nomads of the Russian steppes and Mongolia, not only as a riding horse, but also for its source of a milk supply. A Bashkir horse could give up to six gallons of milk a day, and in Russia today they are used in many areas as a dairy supply.

When Damele learned this, he tried an experiment. Using one of the fur-coated mares that had recently foaled, he took from her almost three gallons of milk on the first milking and more than three gallons on the second.

Damele's investigation further revealed that explorers since the late 1700s had seen the curious breed running with mustangs in Canada, Utah, Nevada, Colorado, and Wyoming. Strangely, however, none has ever been reported in California or the Southwest.

It is easy to understand how these horses could have reached the United States over the land bridge across the Bering Sea from Asia. Many of the Indians of the West have physical characteristics similar to the Mongolians. Add these two speculations, and a theory could be plausible that Ghengis Khan had a few troops exploring his east, at the same time he overran Europe to his west. Thus, in addition to the Romans and the Phoenicians in the western part of the hemisphere, possibly can be added the Mongolian hordes who rode their dairy supply across the Bering Sea bridge. Why not? Even today, the United States is only twenty-two miles from Russia.

Peg Leg knew a lot about the old West, but it is a cinch the one-legged bandit did not know that his mount was similar to one ridden by the greatest bandit the world has ever known—Ghengis Khan.

6

Men Who Have Lost Their Heads

If the ghost of Murrieta still roams the mountains of California seeking his head, then a plethora of ghosts must haunt the wild and sinister Nahanni Valley in Canada's primitive Northwest Territories. Here a known thirteen men have lost their lives, and have mysteriously lost their heads, in a series of murders so strange that not one clue has ever been advanced as to the identity of the culprits. That there is more than one slayer is evident in that the murders have covered a span of more than sixty years. The Nahanni Indians have no doubt as to the identity of the guilty parties. They believe the murderers are a race of hairy demons that frequent the Nahanni Valley, hairy demons who stand as high as a Kodiak bear, are as swift as a bird in flight, and who kill all things they can reach by cutting off their heads. They are known as the Naconni. Their skin is so tough that a bullet will not penetrate it and cutting it with a knife is more difficult than cutting stone.

The area is known by three names: Nahanni Valley, Deadman's Valley, and Headless Valley. It has a unique reputation for three things—a vast supply of gold ore, a lush tropical climate, and sudden and mysterious death. Of these reputations, one is exaggerated, one is true, and the other may be possible.

Headless Valley, its most popular name, is located in an area near the headwaters of the South Nahanni River, not far distant from the Arctic Circle. The valley is flat and verdant, surrounded by tall mountains and filled with hot sulphur

58

springs, some of which make the waters of the South Nahanni run warm even in the coldest season. Often the springs send huge clouds of steam into the air, hiding the sinister valley under a cloak of fog.

Spring always comes first to Headless Valley. Stands of wild timothy, up to seven feet high, burst into bloom while the nearby mountain slopes still are gripped in the hard frozen fist of winter. Wild raspberries, gooseberries, black and red currants, and wild roses grow exuberantly and spread in huge, colorful ribbons across the valley. There are relics of preglacial palms and other tropical flora, but there is no mystery to the reason for this strange temperate island near the Arctic. The land is sub-irrigated by the warm springs and it is this that accounts for the fruits, the near tropical growth of grass, and the black and orange butterflies that flicker among red and yellow columbines. There are even reports that hummingbirds can be seen in Headless Valley. It is indeed a paradox that such a haven for the frostbitten Arctic explorer is avoided like the plague by all but a handful of adventurers.

It has been a taboo to the Nahannis for generations upon generations but, as near as can be determined, its curse first struck the white man shortly after the turn of the century. In January of 1904, three brothers named McLeod—Willie, Frank and Charlie—heard reports in Edmonton, Alberta, that there might be gold in Nahanni Valley and decided to spend the summer prospecting for it. It is unknown whether or not they had ever heard of the Naconni, but if they had, it is reasonable to assume that they would consider it no more than Indian superstition.

Their method of entry has been well documented. The three brothers went first to Vancouver, British Columbia, then caught a ship up the Inland Passage to Wrangell, Alaska. Here the McLeods bought dogs and sleds and other paraphernalia necessary to prospectors exploring the cold north, then chartered a boat to carry them up the Stikine River to a point where the stream was still solidly frozen. It was a long and most arduous trip, a journey of more than a thousand miles, following the frozen streams across British Columbia, the Yukon, and finally into Northwest Territory. Near the Upper Flat River, they came across a group of Cassiar Indians who, Charles McLeod reported later, had nuggets worth about three dollars each in their possession. Because of this, they spent several weeks in this area, searching for the source of the Indian supply. They were unsuccessful, however, and moved on up the Upper Flat River, where, fearful of being trapped by snow, they constructed a raft and floated down the South Nahanni River passing through Headless Valley, until they reached the community of Fort Liard where they elected to spend the winter.

Charles McLeod obtained a job with the Hudson's Bay Company and, possibly because of this, he decided against going back into the Nahanni Valley the following spring. Willie and Frank McLeod enlisted a man named Wilkinson, described in various accounts as an Englishman, a Scotchman, or an Australian, and once again set out in their search for the gold of the Nahanni. It was the spring of 1905.

By the spring of 1908, Charlie McLeod decided that all was not well with his missing brothers and, leaving his job with the Hudson's Bay Company, he set out on a one-man search for them. By the late summer he had given up the search and was following the South Nahanni River back to Fort Liard. On the edge of the warm valley fed by the hot springs he noticed a broken sled runner. On the wood had been written in Willie's handwriting, "We have found a fine prospect." There was no date on the message nor was there any explanation as to why it had been written.

Charlie moved on. About a mile farther down the stream he came across the remains of his two brothers, two skeletons encased only in the remnants of long underwear. Both skeletons were headless. One lay on its back near a spread-out bedroll. The other was on its chest, an arm outstretched toward a rifle which was leaning against a tree about three feet distant. There was no sign of the man known as Wilkinson.

The Nahanni Indians were not surprised. It was taboo to enter the valley because of the Naconni demons who killed their victims by pulling off their heads. The white men around Fort Liard did not dismiss the incident so easily. The Royal Canadian Mounted Police were notified, and they launched a search for the missing Wilkinson, but this proved to be one instance where they did not get their man. There were reports that he had been seen in Vancouver with more than $8,000 worth of gold dust in his possession, but he was never caught, if it were he. The story of the gold, however, spread throughout the Canadian Northwest. The prospectors who scoffed at the Nahanni taboo were quick to believe that the McLeods had found a strike in the valley. Several scouted the area and returned safe but empty-handed.

In 1909, a man named Karl Jorgenson appeared in Pelley Lakes. A prospector, he became friendly with Poole Field, a merchant with a reputation for grubstaking individuals who hunted for gold. It is not known whether or not Field grubstaked Jorgenson, but it is known that the latter was well outfitted when he left for Nahanni Valley to search for the McLeod strike. Field did not hear from Jorgenson for two years, until an Indian appeared at the Field store with a letter from the Swedish prospector whom he had met in the foothills rising from the mysterious valley. In the letter, Jorgenson said that he had struck it rich and asked Field to join him. A map was enclosed showing Field where Jorgenson had built a small cabin along the banks of the South Nahanni River inside Headless Valley.

A few months later Field arrived at the rendezvous. The cabin had been burned to the ground. Lying at a point halfway between the cabin and the bank of the river was Jorgenson's bleached, headless skeleton. There was no sign of clothing on the remains. Near the skeleton was an overturned bucket and still clutched in a bony hand was Jorgenson's Savage rifle from which two shots had been fired.

It was enough to establish firmly the menace of Headless Valley. But the white man by nature is skeptical, and the lure of gold is strong. The value of the McLeod gold strike assumed astronomical proportions as the story was passed around, and the reward appeared to many well worth risking one's head. The parties that went into Headless Valley became larger, but no one found the gold. Most of the searchers returned safely. One group of three did not. Again there were headless skeletons, this time apparently slain as they slept on the banks of the warm South Nahanni. No one knows who they were or how they entered the Headless Valley. There are some that say the three victims never did exist, that they were only the result of a barroom conversation. If so, it acted as no deterrent to the hunters of McLeod's gold.

In 1929, a group of three prospectors named Gilroy, Hay, and Hall entered the sinister paradise on the search. There was a minor squabble and Hall abandoned his companions to continue the search on his own. Hall affected a peculiar type of hobnailed boot, and a few days later, Gilroy and Hay ran across the imprint of the boot in the soft dirt near the bank of the river. This was the last sign of Hall. Not even his headless skeleton has been found, if this macabre death was his fate.

Two years later, a young man named Philip Powers entered the Headless Valley. The purpose of his visit was twofold. He was a trapper and he theorized that the warm valley might be a haven for many fur-bearing animals. While scouting it for this basic purpose, he might possibly find some clues as to the location of the McLeod gold. His fate was almost identical to that of Jorgenson.

In 1931, investigations of disappearances in Headless Valley were launched much more quickly than in the time when the McLeods were killed. Nevertheless, almost a year passed before word reached the Royal Canadian Mounted Police that Powers was long overdue on his return to civilization. It did not take the Mounties long to find him. He had met his death just outside the small cabin he had built along the banks of the river. The cabin had been burned to the ground. His skeleton lay a few feet from the charred embers, a bony index finger curved around the trigger of his revolver. His head was missing.

A man named Lewis Shebbach drifted into Fort Liard in the late spring of 1948, listened to the tales of the Headless Valley, and let the lure of the gold bring him to his death. In the summer of 1949, the Mounties again made their search of the area and once again found a headless skeleton. There were a few differences from the other grisly discoveries. Although minus its head, Shebbach's skeleton was found at a place called Caribou Creek, some distance from the scene of the others, and in this instance the bones were strewn over a fifty-yard area apparently scattered by wild animals.

There have been other headless victims of the Naconni demons in Headless Valley. The story is always the same. Two men named Eppler and Mulholland died in 1936, a man named Holmberg in 1940. The known death toll to date is thirteen plus the three unidentified prospectors, if that tale is true. There undoubtedly have been hundreds who have gone in and come out without the slightest trouble.

Among the latter are three who have thoroughly explored the Headless Valley: Gordon Matthews, Albert Faille, and R. M. Patterson. In 1954, Patterson wrote a book about the Nahanni Valley entitled *Dangerous River* (published by William Sloane Associates). Patterson debunks the entire legend. Citing Shebbach as an example, he wonders why the wild animals who scattered Shebbach's bones failed to do so with the other victims. Still unanswered, however, is what happened to Shebbach's head. Logically, it is easy to assume that the thirteen all died from some unfortunate accident. Jorgenson could have tripped while running to get a bucket of water to put out the fire in his cabin and accidentally have shot himself. The same thing could have happened to Powers. Wilkinson could have shot the McLeods for their gold. As Patterson points out, some could have starved, or died from a heart attack. But what happened to their heads?

In his story of his two journeys through Headless Valley, however, Patterson admits there is something vaguely sinister about the whole of the Headless Valley. It is not clean. It smells of sulphur constantly because of the hot springs, although he says most of the springs are remarkably clear. Although shunned by the Indians today, Patterson discovered signs that it was once inhabited. On the floor of a cave in which he spent a stormy night, he dug through a thin layer of soil and turned up many bones that had been gnawed upon and broken. Mixed with them was a stone arrowhead. He found no skulls in the cave.

The Headless Valley no longer is as remote as when the McLeods set off on their journey from Wrangell, Alaska. The Alcan Highway passes within two hundred miles of the Nahanni, and the trek across the mountains from this point is not a difficult one during the summer.

The legend of the McLeod gold still circulates, but those who hunt for it should be careful not to lose their heads during the search.

7

The Curse of Santa Isabel

A part of the western treasure syndrome are the tales of
lost missions, most of which are reported to be repositories
for incredible amounts of bullion, jeweled gold and silver
icons. No one can dispute the fact that some of the missions
built by the Jesuits have become lost, because their existence
is attested to by records in the files of the Catholic Archdio-
cese in Mexico City and old maps still in existence. An example of the latter is a map in the possession of the Bancroft
Library in Berkeley. The cartographer was Father Eusebio
Francisco Chino, a mysterious Jesuit who used many names
and who perhaps is best known as Father Kino. This particular map, drawn in 1702, clearly marks the location of a
Mission San Dionysius near Yuma on the Colorado River.
One of Father Kino's diaries mentions his visit to this mission, yet today there is no sign that a mission ever existed
here, nor has any other record ever been found attesting to
its existence. There is no mystery, however, as to the reason
for this.

The first missions of the West were founded by zealous
Jesuits. The archivists in the diocese also were Jesuits, and in
the mid-eighteenth century they found themselves suddenly
snared in a political situation that they felt required the
destruction of many mission records. This situation arose
when the king of Spain became suspicious of the burgeoning
power wielded in New Spain by the Jesuits and abruptly
ordered them all expelled, to be replaced by the more docile
Franciscan padres. Understandably, the Jesuits were reluctant

to give up the extensive property of their own order. Hoping for what now is called "a change in administration," they efficiently and systematically destroyed as many records as possible pertaining to their property and removed the most valuable of their treasures from their many churches and missions for what they believed would be temporary storage in safe hiding spots.

They were most successful. It is significant that in a land of plundered Incan gold the inventories made by the arriving Franciscans showed a notable lack of gold icons acquired by the Jesuits. Candlesticks, vessels, altars, and other churchly appointments were described by the Franciscans as made of silver and other inferior metals, yet all Spanish records of the times referred to the golden opulence of the Jesuit order and its sudden disappearance.

It is upon this historical note that the legend of the Lost Mission of Santa Isabel is based, a legend worth telling because of the tragic experience of a young adventuresome Scotsman about forty-five years ago and its relationship to the curse that surrounds the lost mission. Even today the curse strikes terror in the hearts of the Yaqui Indians of the Southwest. The Yaquis call it *El Maldeción de Isabel*— Isabel's curse.

According to the legend, several of the Jesuit churches along the western coast of Mexico, from San Blas to Mazatlan, gathered up their gold from dozens of churches and impressed about fifty Yaqui Indians into service to load the treasure on a small Spanish ship at San Blas. Twenty-five of the most faithful converts among the Yaquis were taken on the ship to act as stevedores and porters when the ship reached its destination—the Mission of Santa Isabel.

The treasure was unloaded from the ship in small boats several days later, and the Yaqui porters carried it overland to the mission. Stories vary here. Some say the precious metals and jewels were buried in the walls of the adobe mission. Others say it was buried on the grounds or in a small cave adjacent to the mission. But the legends agree that, after the treasure was secreted, the priest in charge of the expedition lined the Yaqui porters up in drill formation.

"This is the treasure of the Lord," the padre intoned. "He will guard His offerings and he who would disturb this sanctuary or tell anyone else of this sanctuary will be the object of His wrath. The Lord will smite him dead no sooner than the words are uttered or the desecration attempted."

The superstitious Indians planted cacti and scrub trees in the path to the Mission Santa Isabel, and all signs of the trail leading to the mission were obliterated. The priests, including those who had been stationed in the remote mission, sailed back to San Blas and the Yaquis drifted away, each carrying with him a tale of the curse placed upon the person who would attempt to recover the treasure.

Years later—the time element is most vague—a Yaqui Indian was foraging in a wilderness mountain area. He came to the base of a tall cliff, and as he walked around it he spotted what appeared to be the remnants of an old trail. Following it, he scaled the side of the mountain and came out on a small plain. He skirted the edge of the mesa for a short distance, then paused. Far down below him was a narrow canyon and in a hidden valley at the end of the canyon stood a large building . . . a church. Chaparral grew near the door; bells hung on cross bars in apertures built over the roof on both sides of a barred door. In the rear of the building he saw a cluster of natural water tanks. There were three large palm trees, and large plots of arrowhead and tobacco plants.

Possibly the Yaqui had heard of the curse of the Isabel Mission, for he studied the hidden area carefully, then withdrew. By nightfall he was back in his village.

It is equally possible that he did not know the scope of the curse. That night, around the campfire, he related to his fellow tribesmen his adventures of the day. No sooner had he finished than he leaped to his feet. For perhaps half a minute he clutched his throat. Then with a loud cry, he spun around and dropped dead before his tribe.

There is not a Yaqui in all of Mexico who does not know of the story today. And if any Yaqui ever has stumbled on to the Mission of Santa Isabel, he has turned his back quickly and said nothing of it to a soul. Indian superstition, one could say, but there is a most strange sequel to the curse of the Mission Santa Isabel.

Shortly after World War I, a young man with the unimaginative native name of David Jamison, a native of Scotland, drifted into Tucson, Arizona. Jamison had heard many tales of lost mines and buried treasure in the southwestern section of the United States and he decided to have a fling at prospecting for some of it. For several months he roamed through the nearby mountains, turning up nothing, but enjoying himself immensely.

Jamison had a little money, apparently, as all of his trips were well equipped. He was a careful man and when he expected to be gone more than a week, he arranged to have a friend named Bill Walters drive out to a predetermined meeting spot with additional supplies. By the fall of the year, Jamison was centering his exploration in the Pajarito Mountains.

This range is on the border between Arizona and Sonora, Mexico, where the international boundary makes a sharp angle toward the northwest and the Gulf of California. Not too far distant from the gulf there is a high mountain known as Cerro Ruido, or Noisy Mountain. The range roughly parallels the border, starting at a point near both Nogaleses and running toward the west for about twenty-five miles. They form a high gabled roof along the border, and although parched desert bleeds away from the mountains on both sides, within the range itself there are many small springs that run through the rocky valleys and narrow canyons before disappearing in some subterranean channel to empty into the gulf or the Colorado River.

In the early summer of 1922, Jamison established a camp in the foothills of the Pajarito Mountains not far from the end of the last dim road leading southward from a ranch of Don Felipe and within view of the ominous cliffs of Cerro Ruido. He was warned to be careful as the area was considered treacherous, one that was even shunned by Yaqui Indians.

Jamison was driven into his camp by Walters, who helped him set it up before he departed. A week later Walters returned with new supplies. Jamison was in high spirits. The day before, somt ten miles into the mountains, he had run across what appeared to be an ancient trail, he told Walters. It had been late in the afternoon, and not wishing to be caught out of his base camp by dark, he had returned. In the morning he planned to follow it. He was convinced the trail would lead to some lost mine.

Walters went back to Tucson. A week later, on schedule, he returned once again to Jamison's base camp with another truckload of supplies. As he drove up the road he noticed big thunderheads gathering in the mountains above him and occasionally a clap of thunder bounced off the face of Cerro Ruido.

When he arrived in the camp, Jamison was asleep. It was obvious that something had happened to the amiable Scot, for his clothes were torn and his face and arms badly scratched. Jamison awoke as Walters approached. The Scot was highly elated and immediately launched into a recounting of his adventure.

The day after the two men had parted a week earlier, Jamison once again had located the almost invisible trail. It led to the base of a high cliff at the foot of Cerro Ruido, then picked its way up the mountain. Halfway to the top, he had come out onto a high mesa, where he lost the trail. Cerro Ruido veered sharply above him and knowing that the path could go no higher, Jamison skirted the edge of the mesa, searching for a spot in which the trail possibly dipped downward again. It was then he saw the small canyon where, pinched in the end of the narrow breech, was a building that obviously was a mission.

On top of the building were four belfry portals without bells. The face of the building was made of white stone, similar to the smooth walls of the canyon. A solitary palm tree jutted into the sky to the right and rear of the building. Chaparral and mesquite covered the area.

For a long time he stared at the building almost in disbelief. Then, once again, he started to look for the path that would take him down into the canyon. He could find none, although he spent the remainder of the day searching. The next day he raced back to the mesa shortly after dawn. By noon he was convinced that there was no way down into the canyon from this side.

This night, when he returned to his base camp, he packed his knapsack, and the following morning, using bearings taken the day previously, he veered around a small sawtooth finger of the range and came up on the canyon from the rear. It took him a long time to force his way through the thick scrub and underbrush, but eventually he cut his way into the canyon. By the time he was in the entrance to the canyon, it was night, and unrolling his bedding he prepared to sleep. He had no desire to fall into some forgotten mine shaft or a rotted wine cellar.

He had no idea how long he had been lying on his blankets staring at the black profile of the ancient church in the moonlight. But just as he was dropping off to sleep, he heard a blood-curdling scream, so loud that he involuntarily leaped to his feet.

He froze with a fear he had never before experienced. A moment later he saw movement at the building. It was then he panicked and ran headlong up the canyon. The scrub ripped and tore his clothes, scratching his body. He ran only a short distance, then sanity returned abruptly and he halted and turned. Then he laughed. Silhouetted against the moon, reminding him of a cardboard cutout for a Halloween decoration, was a large wildcat.

Jamison returned to his bed, where eventually his nerves quieted and he fell asleep. In the morning he explored the abandoned church. Around noon he passed a smooth section of the canyon wall, a few yards distant from the mission, and felt a breath of cool air. There was a small hole in the wall and upon examining it, Jamison decided that it came from a crack between two stones. A moment later he discovered something more sensational. The stones had been mortared to cover a much larger hole, approximately six feet tall and three feet wide.

He tried to enlarge it with the small trench shovel carried in his pack but succeeded only in chipping away a few inches. Peering through it, he glimpsed "scores of rotting leather bags." He could see no more than this, nor, despite his almost frenzied attempts to pry the hole larger, could he loosen the mortared stones. Eventually he gave up. This would be a job for pick and stone chisel.

Before he left to return to his base camp and await Walters' next arrival, Jamison did one more thing. Removing a small camera from his knapsack, he photographed the front of the mission, the hole he had chopped in the sealed entrance to the cave, and the crumbling walls of another building that once apparently had been joined to the main edifice.

This was the story Jamison told Walters when the latter awakened him in the base camp. About an hour later, Walters started the engine of his truck, promising to return the next day with large picks, dynamite, and stone chisels. As he started to turn, Jamison reached in his pocket and passed Walters the roll of film. "Will you drop these off at the photo shop and get them developed for me?" he asked.

Walters promised he would. Jamison said he would scout

a shorter route into the canyon while he was waiting for Walters to return.

The thunderheads began to gather before Walters was out of the foothills. The angry thunder bounced off the ominous Cerro Ruido with such force that the small pickup truck vibrated. When Walters reached the Don Felipe ranch, he stopped and looked back. The storm was one of the most severe he had ever seen in the Pajarito Mountains. Lightning raced from peak to peak and streaked down to the earth in giant fingers from the angry heavens.

Walters also had a camera. He took a picture of the driving storm. He was not worried about Jamison. The Scotsman was a cautious man and well versed in mountain "savvy." Walters climbed back into his truck and drove on into Tucson.

He left the film in a shop, ordered the necessary supplies, and then went to his home. That night the storm swept out of the mountains, raced across the desert and whipped the city. Up to this time, it was the worst storm in the history of the Tucson weather bureau. Nogales, Mexico, and Nogales, Arizona, reported damage of more than a half-million dollars.

But by morning, the land once again was peaceful. Walters left Tucson at eight A.M. to return to the base camp. It took him much longer than usual to reach it, and when he did, there was nothing left. The rocks and boulders that had slowed him on the dim road leading into the forbidding Cerro Ruido had all come down the wide canyon and across the small level area where Jamison had pitched his base camp. There was not a sign of the Scot, nothing to indicate any human ever had been in the area. In place of the flat camping spot was a huge scar, furrowed across the field. Walters knew at once what had happened. A tremendous flash flood had swept down the canyon, the water sweeping across the area as if spewed from a ruptured dam.

A search was launched for Jamison. There was no sign of him. A few days later, some three miles down the road, Walters found a small frying pan that looked like the one Jamison had carried with him. It was bent double, like a clam shell.

Almost a month later, Walters remembered the pictures he had given to the photographer.

They all turned out with professional clarity. There was

the picture of the mission, the crumbling walls, the small hole Jamison had chopped in the wall.

Walters spent months looking for the canyon and so have scores of other persons. The search has been conducted by plane and jeep and horseback, as well as on foot. As far as anyone knows, the mission still remains hidden.

Could Jamison have been a victim of Isabel's Curse?

The lost mission of Santa Isabel has for years been presumed to be somewhere in Baja, much farther to the west and south. Another old Jesuit map, drawn in 1757, shows an Isabel a few miles south of the fishing port of San Felipe in Baja. One of the writers spent several days exploring this area, but found nothing to indicate the site of an ancient mission marked "Isabel."

It is an interesting speculation that the hidden mission in the Pajarito Mountains is indeed the long lost Santa Isabel Mission. The ship carrying the Jesuits and the Yaquis easily could have sailed within portage distance of the Pajaritos and the Indians from San Blas would not have known whether they were in Baja or San Gabriel.

Not to be overlooked is Isabel's Curse and the sudden death of an adventuresome Scot named David Jamison.

8

A Few Haunted Houses

There are buildings throughout the Southwest that were old before the Pilgrims landed on Plymouth Rock. Some of these, made out of no more than mud and straw, adobe, still are lived in, or house expensive restaurants so old that title insurance companies could not report with certainty when they were constructed or by whom.

Some are comparatively recent, not more than a century old, and of such odd architecture and in such unexpected locations that one would be convinced they were focal points of legends or stories. In the decaying community of Austin, Nevada, once a flourishing mining city, there is Stokes Castle. Perched on top of a tall hill, it is visible for miles, a perfectly square granite structure rising high into the sky. It has been abandoned for years. The floors have rotted out. The occasional tourist racing across the desert in the center of the state may stop to take a snapshot, but if he can find anyone around to ask its history, he can be given its entire historical background in one sentence.

"A man named Stokes built it back when the mines were working and when the mines folded, he moved away."

In the Santa Clara Valley, near San Jose, California, there is a huge rambling structure known as the Winchester House. It was never completed, although artisans, contractors, and carpenters worked on it daily for more than a quarter century. It was owned by the widow of the late arms manufacturer, who, after the death of her husband and daughters, sought escape from reality through the science of seance. A medium convinced her that she would not die until the house was completed. The fortune teller was wrong, although it took more than twenty-five years to prove it. The house is open to the public still unfinished.

Perhaps one of the most intriguing houses in the West, however, is a huge, four-story brick and granite mansion in the ghost town of White Oaks, New Mexico. This house was built as a direct outgrowth of an old Mexican legend, but unlike the Mexican legend, the ending was not a happy one.

The Mexican legend concerns a building that until recently was used to house the *Secretaria de Communicaciones*. It was completed on June 28, 1731, during the Spanish regime, and was constructed as a customs house. However, before it was completed, work on the building had been underway for decades with little more progress than the laying of the foundation.

Living in Mexico City at this time was a wealthy Spanish playboy named Don Juan Gutiérrez Rubin de Celis. He was so rich that he had no idea of his own holdings, and at the inauguration of the Duque de Arion as the new viceroy, Don Juan spent 30,000 pesos on a greatcoat covered with precious stones. But in addition to his wealth, Don Juan enjoyed another reputation . . . that of the laziest man in New Spain.

When in his mid-forties, Don Juan fell in love with a beautiful teenage senorita, Doña Sara de García Somera y Acuña. Despite the difference in years, she apparently thought him eminently qualified as a suitor except for his reputation for laziness. As Don Juan grew more ardent in his suit, Doña Sara decided to put him to test. If Don Juan would supervise the construction of the customs house, she proposed, and give the building completed, with the keys delivered to the viceroy, within six months, she would indeed marry him.

Don Juan accepted the provisions, and despite warnings from every one of his friends that the stipulation was impossible, he started work. At his own expense, he imported an army of workers from as far away as Vera Cruz, paid fantastic sums to architects and carpenters and personally supervised, day and night, the erection of the building. Three days before the deadline, the building was completed, its interior immaculate, and the keys delivered to the viceroy. The banns were posted and in the proper time, Doña Sara became the bride of Don Juan.

A plaque on the building still remains:

> *Siendo prior del Consulado el coronel Don Juan*
> *Gutiérrez Rubin de Celis, caballero del*
> *Orden de Santiago, y, consules Dn.*
> *Garza de Alvarado del mismo Orden, y, Dn. Lucas.*
> *Serafín Chacón, se acabo la Fabrica de esta.*
> *Aduaña en 28 de Junio de 1731.*

It is an acrostic inscription. The first letters of the lines are the initials of Doña Sara de García Somera y Acuna.

Almost 150 years later a young American from Cincinnati, Ohio, paused in a cantina in White Oaks, New Mexico, for a glass of beer. His name was Roger Bates and, like Don Juan, he was very wealthy. He owned the smelter in White Oaks, the only one for hundreds of miles, and his earnings exceeded the combined incomes of the owners of gold mines in the area. Like Don Juan, he was approaching his forties. Like Don Juan, he was very much in love with a girl yet to see twenty.

The town of White Oaks was built much more substantially than other mining towns of the West in the mid-nineteenth century. The same hills that produced the gold, and there was a plethora of it, also produced huge amounts of granite. Then, as now, lumber was a scarce item in this community adjoining the great White Sands Desert, and all that was brought in was needed for the mines. Thus the commercial establishments along the main street, the bank, the hotels, the jail, and even the brothel were built of granite.

As Roger Bates sipped his beer, he sat at a table next to a group of Mexican miners. One of them was an older man, a storyteller, and he was recounting the tale of Don Juan and the customs house of Santo Domingo.

When Roger Bates left the cantina and returned to his suite in the hotel, he could not help but draw a parallel between himself and the fabled Spanish aristocrat. About the only difference he could see was that Don Juan was not separated from his beloved by more than fifteen hundred miles, and approximate distance between White Oaks, New Mexico, and Cincinnati, Ohio. But soon he would be returning to Cincinnati, he quite possibly reflected, to claim his bride. He had come to the West almost penniless a few years earlier and now he was rich enough to abandon all work for the rest of his life if he so desired.

It was late spring when Roger Bates returned to his home in Ohio. And it is reasonable to assume that he had been there but a very short time before he made his proposal.

His beloved, however, was very cool to his plans to take her back to the Wild West. Only the other day, the local papers had carried a story to the effect that Billy the Kid had broken out of the jail at White Oaks, killing a man in his escape. Besides, where would they live? He certainly could not expect her to live in a hotel.

It was then that Roger Bates recalled the story of Don Juan's courtship. "Give me a year," he said, "and I will build you the finest house between St. Louis and Los Angeles." His beloved agreed and demurely accepted the large diamond ring to signify the engagement and the promise.

Roger Bates returned to White Oaks and immediately began construction of the finest house between St. Louis and Los Angeles. Because, in his opinion, brick was more attractive than granite, he constructed a brickyard in White Oaks and imported labor from as far off as Juárez, Mexico, to operate it.

The huge basement was built of granite. In each of the thirty-one rooms, the floors were laid of hardwood and the tile in each of the thirty-one fireplaces was imported terrazzo brought from Italy. The heavy and expensive furnishings were shipped overland from New York. The house, finished in ten months, was on the highest point of land in White Oaks, and if it was not the grandest between Missouri and California, it quite probably was one of the most expensive.

The following spring an eager Roger Bates departed for Cincinnati. He carried with him a large oil painting of the house, painted by an artist brought down from Santa Fe. The smelter and the mines shut down on the day he left for there was not a soul in the city of White Oaks who was not aware of the great love of Roger Bates. Not a soul in White Oaks ever saw Roger Bates again.

Again three months after his departure, a Harry Bates, his wife, and their only daughter arrived in White Oaks and moved into the great mansion. Harry, as taciturn as Roger was gregarious, carried papers signed by his brother Roger in which he had been granted title to both the smelter and the house. Harry told a banker, who pressed him for details, that when Roger arrived in Cincinnati he found his beloved had married another man and was about ready to deliver her first child.

Harry Bates and his family had lived in the house less than a week when tragedy struck. His only daughter wandered off into the hills. When a searching party found her several hours later she was dead of a rattlesnake bite. It was too much for Harry Bates and his grief-stricken wife. The day after the funeral they abandoned the house. And, as if this were the portent of things to come, a shaft in one of the largest mines caved in, killing a half-dozen miners.

The community deteriorated rapidly. The other mines closed down as the veins were emptied. The merchants and the bankers and the prostitutes drifted away. By the turn of the century, the largest city in notorious Lincoln County, which boasted at its peak more than eight thousand residents, had shrunk to less than one hundred. But unlike other ghost towns throughout the West, the buildings in White Oaks did not rot and collapse and disappear. They were built of granite, and one on the hill, made of granite and brick, had been built to last for generations.

The community and the house still stand. A narrow road, that can be traversed by a jeep, runs the sixteen miles between the ghost city and Carrizozo, a small city on the edge of the White Sands Proving Ground. Possibly because the buildings still stand with little signs of wear, White Oaks, unlike other ghost cities, is still listed on the maps of New Mexico. Recently its only inhabitant was an ancient Negro sheepherder who settled near the two scrub white oaks from which the town drew its name.

The doors and windows are gone from the unlived-in Bates House, and so is most of the furniture brought at such expense from New York. In the basement there is a row of deep shelves and on one of these is an ancient coffin, its lid tightly nailed shut. The sheepherder did not know how the coffin got there nor whether or not it was empty. As far as he knew, it might contain the remains of a small young girl who was bitten by a rattlesnake many years ago.

There are not many old houses, however, in the western part of the United States. Unlike New England, where Victorian widow-walks still overlook the sea, or in the deep South where a form of ancestor worship remains popular, a house in the metropolitan areas of the West rarely survives the length of its original mortgage. Those that do, particularly in southern California, where dwelling longevity is the lowest, appear to strain for some form of recognition before they succumb to a freeway, a parking lot, or new office building.

An example is the Beverly Hills house of writer Joe Hyams and his actress wife Elke Sommers. Their home was built after World War II. It already acquired a ghost who delights in moving furniture around, opening windows, and lurking in doorways. There is, however, an old house with a much older ghost, located in a very remote area of the mysterious Baja Peinsula. It is known as *El Barril,* and there is a strange relationship between it and the stairless two-story dwellings that can still be found in southern Utah.

In southern Utah, there are houses of such an unconventional appearance that they are a mystery to all but those who still live in them, or in the area, or are familiar with early Mormon customs. The peculiar aspect of these large houses is in the number of second- and third-story exterior doors which open onto nothing. A person stepping through one of these doors would fall from twelve to twenty-four feet to the ground.

These homes were built to house the large families of the polygamous early Mormon settlers. It was custom for a Mormon patriarch to live with his first wife and family on the ground floor. Additional wives, and the children they bore, lived in individual apartments on the higher floors and originally each apartment opened onto a balcony with a staircase to the ground, or else each apartment had its own stairway to the ground level.

When Brigham Young, the president of the Mormon Church, received his heavenly directive to forgo the custom of polygamy, he ordered all outward manifestations of the practice to be destroyed. The extra wives and their children were moved to separate quarters, and the exterior stairways and balconies to their former apartments were ripped off the buildings as proof to the nation that the new order was being observed.

It left the owner of the building in a peculiar situation. Because the homes contained no interior stairs, the upper floors were now inaccessible, and the owner of a large three-story house found himself restricted to the ground floor. There are many tales of splendid cherrywood cabinets or heavy maple hutchery, some carried across the prairies in covered wagons, that still remained sealed in these abandoned upper stories.

The haunted house at El Barril in Baja is similar in design to the polygamy houses of southern Utah although the house is more than a thousand miles south of Utah. It is on a remote beach facing the Gulf of California, an impressive three-story stone building with a series of sturdy doors that once opened onto an encircling balcony. Today all of the doors on the upper story are locked, their latches permanently rusted. The balcony encircling the building is partially rotted away, effectively discouraging a visit to the upper floors.

The ground floor is easily accessible. The heavy door opens with only a slight squeak of protest into an enormous room. Leading off this are two smaller rooms, one of which contains a dilapidated billiard table, the felt on the banks and the slate long since rotted away.

It is known that this house at El Barril has been used as a headquarters for pearl smugglers. The same pearl beds that started Juan de Iturbe on his fantastic desert voyage were in these waters, called by the Spanish the Vermillion Sea. From the turn of the century until oysters were wiped out by a disease in 1919, remote little bays of the Vermillion Sea provided a paradise for illicit pearlers seeking a tax-free atmosphere. Mountains of eroded oyster shells around El Barril point up the use of the building as a pearl smuggler's headquarters.

In the back of El Barril is a long flat section of land that passes the building and ends at the gulf. This area is now sparsely covered with dry brush and cacti, but it once was a primitive landing strip for airplanes. Prior to World War II, the Mexican government decreed it illegal to export live lobsters from Mexican waters to markets above the border. North Americans, however, delighted in the taste of the Mexican lobster and paid a much higher price for the delicacy than did the gourmets of Mexico City. Thus El Barril once again became a headquarters for smugglers. Mexican pilots, known as "bug pilots," cleared rocks from level stretches along the gulf where they could land their rickety planes on prearranged schedules to pick up lobster from the fishermen and fly it over the border into California. One of these bug pilots was a man half-Japanese and half-Mexican named Juan Kawakuchi.

Shortly before dusk on an early fall day in 1939, he landed his light aircraft on the crude runway at El Barril and discovered there had been a misunderstanding over the date of his arrival. He was expected on the following day, and the lobsters he was to smuggle back into the United States were still in their traps in the gulf. He had a choice of either remaining overnight at El Barril, which was dangerous because of the Mexican police patrols, or making a round trip empty to his home in Tijuana, which was expensive. He chose to remain overnight. El Barril could be reached only by an ancient trail through a rugged, mountainous pass. It was unlikely an official would show up there. Shortly after dark, Kawakuchi spread out his sleeping bag on the beach.

Some time later he awakened, his face wet from a rare desert drizzle. Carrying his bag, he sought shelter in El Barril, this time stretching out his bag on top of the billiard table, the only piece of furniture inside the building. Again he fell asleep and again he was awakened, this time by the yelping of a small dog. For awhile he lay quietly. The drizzle had stopped, and through the open door he saw the light of the full moon reflected in a wide path across the water of the gulf. The dog seemed more excited. His barking grew louder. Then suddenly Kawakuchi leaped from the billiard table. He remembered distinctly shutting the door to the building before he went to sleep, pulling on it, and the sound of scurrying mice as it screeched into place. Yet now it was wide open.

The dog's yelps became louder and more frenzied. Then in the light of the moon there appeared the shadowy outline of a man and, racing around him, jumping in the air, was a small dog. The stranger raised his arm and brought it down slowly in a stiffened position, as if taking aim. Kawakuchi fired. Both the man and the dog vanished instantly. At the same moment everything grew black. No longer was there light from the moon dancing on the water, nor was the sand on the beach visible. Kawakuchi could smell gunpowder. He could hear ringing in his ears from the noise of the explosion, but he could see nothing. Approaching panic, he thought he had suddenly gone blind and would be unable to fly the plane out in the morning. Turning, he groped along the billiard table for his flashlight. He pressed its switch. He could see.

With a tremendous sigh of relief, he pointed the beam toward the door. It was closed. In its center was a small splintered hole, drilled by the bullet he had fired. Still not trusting his senses, he went over to it. It was fresh, no splinters showed signs of weathering. He kicked open the door. The light came back as it had been, the reflection of the moon casting a wide path across the waters of the gulf. There was no sign of the stranger nor of his dog. Kawakuchi was nonplused. How could he see through a closed door? The bug pilot was not superstitious. There could be only one answer. He had experienced one hell of a bad dream. He picked up his sleeping bag, went back to the beach, and soon was asleep.

The following morning, after the lobsters were brought ashore and they were loading the plane, Kawakuchi told the fishermen of his strange dream. They nodded, knowingly. It was not a dream he had experienced, they explained. Kawakuchi had seen the ghost of Señor Viernes who always appeared on the night of a full moon to tell anyone who slept at El Barril of his murder. Sometimes, he even pointed toward the location of his treasure. Kawakuchi told of shooting at the stranger and the fishermen laughed. No bullet could ever kill a ghost, they said.

It was a case of patricide. Years before, after the pearl smugglers departed, El Barril and the land around it had been squatted on by Señor Viernes and his two sons. He planted the land and raised goats. Some fifty kilometers distant was the town of El Arco. Periodically it was the duty of the sons to carry goat cheese to the store there. It was a long trip. The cheese was packed in crates woven of cactus fiber and strapped to burros. It was an easy life for Señor Viernes. He was an old man who in the springtime thought only of the beauty of the thousands of wild carnations and blue lupines that covered the desert floor. The fancy of his sons, however, turned to other things.

It was on such a day that the elder son, Pedro, became ill and the younger, Manuelo, was forced to carry the cheese to El Arco by himself. Several days later he returned to El Barril accompanied by a black-eyed beauty named Josefina whom, he announced, he had married in El Arco.

Josefina was a calculating wench. She deduced quickly that Señor Viernes lived on a higher standard than he could afford through the sale of goat cheese in El Arco every three months. She pumped her new husband for information. Señor Viernes, she learned, often went as far away as Santa Rosalia, and once even to Mexicali, and returned with large supplies and city clothing for his sons. She learned also that prior to these trips, Señor Viernes disappeared into the nearby mountains for a full day and that, when he returned, the muffled clink of many coins resounded from his pockets.

A few weeks later Josefina peeked from her second-floor bedroom shortly after sunrise. Below, she saw Señor Viernes slap his thigh to beckon his dog and then head for the mountains. All day she chided and scolded and scorned her husband for not demanding his rightful share of the fortune his father had found in the hills. Manuelo, a young man of small mind, eventually became convinced he was being swindled by his father; that if given his rightful share of the treasure, he and Josefina could move into El Arco and live in the grand manner.

It was well into the evening when Señor Viernes returned to El Barril. The moon was full and cast a bright path along the waters of the gulf. He came along the beach, then cut up toward the house in the beam of the room, his dog bounding around his feet. Manuelo waited by the door, thinking furiously of his father's chicanery, then walked toward him, meeting him halfway between the gulf and the house. The discussion did not end in the manner for which Josefina had hoped. Instead of demanding the location of the hidden treasure, Manuelo struck his father on the head with a bung hammer. The blow proved fatal to the old man. Manuelo then removed a handful of gold coins from his father's pockets and fled with his scolding wife to El Arco. Soon they were followed by a sorrowful Pedro who, upon his arrival, notified the Mexican authorities of the crime.

The lobster fishermen did not know what happened to Manuelo and Josefina, nor to Pedro. None of them ever returned to El Barril. The goats that run wild in the nearby mountains are descended from Señor Viernes' herd. Whenever the moon is full, however, the ghost of Señor Viernes returns to El Barril. He is always accompanied by his dog and he always raises his arm, but whether it is to point in the direction of the lost treasure or to ward off the blow from the bung hole hammer is not known.

When Hoover Dam was built across the erratic Colorado River at Boulder, Nevada, a short distance from Las Vegas, the back-up waters formed what is now known as Lake

Mead. It inundated many farms, the entire community of St. Thomas, and an area long abandoned but known as Fort Callville. The fort was named after a Mormon pioneer named Anson Call who, under orders from Brigham Young, oversaw the construction of a mammoth, rock-walled warehouse and an extraordinarily large building for his residence.

Fort Callville came into being around the 1860's and was constructed under great difficulties by brethren of the nearby Muddy River Mission. Although rock was readily available near the barren site, the men had to make their own lime of limestone hauled from miles away. To obtain timber for roofing and woodwork, they had to cut down trees and haul them some eighty miles from Mount Charleston, west of Las Vegas.

This was during a time when relations between the Mormon state of Deseret and the United States Government were extremely strained. Mormon sympathies were on the side of the Confederacy during the Civil War. The Saints lived polygamously, which offered a safe crusade for politicians of the time to carry back to their constituency and, in some circles, Mormon independency was looked upon as another form of secession. Since its inception, the Mormon Church has sent proselytizing missionaries all around the world. Their efforts have been remarkably successful. In the mid-nineteenth century, Mormon missionaries were particularly active in Europe, not only in the art of conversion, but also in their ability to persuade converts to move to Zion, the temporary capital of Mormonism at Salt Lake City.

As the split widened between the United States and Deseret, the Mormons discovered that anticipated freight shipments from the East often mysteriously disappeared. More serious, however, was their discovery that many of their converts to Mormonism from Europe were being met at the docks by competing missionaries and being reconverted before they could get away from the eastern seaboard. It was to combat this desperate situation that Brigham Young ordered the construction of Fort Callville.

No longer would European converts be sent to Salt Lake City via New York or Boston. Instead, they would travel by way of Vera Cruz or Panama, thence overland to the Pacific, and then transported up the Gulf of California to the Colorado River and Fort Callville. From there, wagon trains would carry them the remaining five hundred miles to Salt Lake City.

When Fort Callville was completed, Anson Call discovered that the Colorado River was navigable this far north only during certain times of the year. Although his storerooms were completed in February, it would be two or three months before any freight would arrive to be stored in them. Steamboats made regular runs to the mines of El Dorado, Hardyville, and La Paz and other points to the south along the Colorado River. Above El Dorado, however, they had to be ring-winched through the rapids of the treacherous Black Canyon, and during many months of the year the waters were either too high and swift or too low to permit reasonably safe navigation. The best they could achieve was a couple of trips a month during May and June and possibly three trips monthly from July to November. Thus, other plans for storing merchandise and housing converts brought up the gulf were needed.

At first it was believed that gentiles, the term of the Mormon Church for all who are not of their faith, at El Dorado would cooperate by storing goods and housing converts. It was not a valid assumption. The good citizens of El Dorado hijacked the Mormon freight as readily as did the citizens of the United States.

"The ports below seem to be jealous of the Mormon port," one steamboat captain wrote to the Deseret *News*.

The Mormons then tried to make arrangements at the commercial harbor in Mazatlan, Mexico, but graft and problems with port officials rendered this impractical. The Mormon hierarchy had no choice but to make an independent arrangement along the Gulf of California for housing the converts and storing supplies until such time as they could be moved north. The project was carried out in the utmost secrecy. In fact, so few records were kept and these so ambiguous that many Mormons and historians doubt to this day that the second outpost actually was built. There is reference, however, that a German convert from the Muddy Mission, who had helped in the construction of Fort Callville, was placed in charge of such a project. These plans called for construction of a three-story building with rooms opening only to an exterior balcony and stairs, typical of Mormon establishments of that time. The first floor of the building, opening to the gulf, was to be used as the warehouse; the upper floors would house the converts.

The rift between the United States and the State of Deseret widened until it resulted in a debacle that is glossed over in the annals of the U.S. Army. Washington dispatched an army under the command of General Johnson to wipe out the Mormons and make the world safe for monogamy. Johnson's army, however, was wiped out by the Mormons when it was ambushed in a canyon east of Salt Lake City. The victorious Mormons realized that their victory would be of a temporary nature and that a larger army would soon follow the incompetent Johnson. Thus came the revelation to Brigham Young that banned polygamy. The United States quit hijacking the Mormon freight and the European Mormon converts no longer were met by indignant evangelists when they arrived in New York.

At the same time, the tracks of Mark Hopkins' Central Pacific Railroad were nearing those of the Union Pacific and it was most evident to the Mormon leadership that cross-country rail transportation was much more practical than the river transportation up the Colorado. Consequently, Fort Callville was abandoned and eventually became inundated by the waters of Lake Mead. Fortunately, pictures of the old Mormon fort survived its drowning. Pictures have also been taken by one of the writers of this book of the haunted house at El Barril while on an expedition to Baja with Erle Stanley Gardner, the explorer-writer.

The house of Anson Call at Fort Callville and the house at El Barril are almost identical. Each was built of rock and mortar. Each has a distinctive keystone design above the door openings and each has the same type of milled doors. The presumption that it was built by the Mormons as a station for the European converts coming up the gulf is a logical one.

The legend of Señor Viernes, the kindly old man done to death by his son, says that Viernes had found his financial security when he discovered a lost mission full of coins. Some say the lost mission was the Santa Isabel and that Viernes was a victim of its curse.

It is ironic that the lost Mormon way station might have been built on the property of the Jesuits. It is enough to make the old padres roll over in their graves.

9

The City in Which Nobody Lives

Most of the ghost towns throughout the West have a common history. A mine was discovered and this brought the miners who in turn brought the merchants, the gamblers, and the prostitutes. When the mines became barren, the towns died quickly. Many vanished completely. Some still linger on, like a bed-ridden old man. There are some in Nevada where old timers still congregate in the single saloon of the community and talk optimistically of the boom that will return as soon as the price of silver goes up and it becomes profitable to work the mines again. Some others have survived because the land could be farmed as well as mined.

Some not only have survived, but also have achieved a greater prosperity than they enjoyed at the peak of the '49 gold rush. The city of Jackson, next to Sutter's Creek in California's Mother Lode Country, is an example. It has changed very little within the past century. Bearded cowboys still hook their high-heeled boots over the rail of a saloon. The sound of gunfire in the streets is not uncommon. Horses still are tethered to hitching posts. Gambling is still legal, and the card dealers keep the cuffs of their shirts raised high by fancy garters over their biceps. It is all a façade. The bullets are blanks. The barroom fights are staged. Behind the false fronts of the buildings sit the shrewd men of the Chamber of Commerce who have learned that more profit can be made from the tourists of Los Angeles and San Francisco than ever was made from the gold taken from the miners. In the state of Oregon, however, there is a ghost town that to a large extent is owned by southern Californians, a fact that has resulted in an almost continual headache for the fathers of Curry County in which it is located. It quite probably is one of the largest and shortest-lived ghost cities in the West.

On a pleasant summer day in 1915 an elderly man by the name of Charles Neff picked up his rifle and strolled unmolested around the streets of Lakeport, Oregon. Before the day was done, he had wiped out one-third of the town by dispatching one Curly Wittman with two well placed shots. The remaining third, a gentleman by the name of James Murphey, left the Lakeport Hotel where he had been living at no cost, slipped out of town and never returned. Neff apparently then went wading in Floras Lake, the body of water which gave the town its name, where his body was discovered a week later by a passing deputy sheriff. Curry County officials shook their heads over the incident, then breathed a collective sigh of relief thinking that this tragedy surely marked the end of a painful, multi-million-dollar promotion dreamed up by a couple of confidence men many years earlier.

The site of Lakeport is one of the most beautiful in Oregon. Floras Lake is large and deep and abundant with fish. At its western end is a sandbar between three and four hundred yards long that shelves sharply down to the Pacific, separating the lake from the ocean. In the late summer of 1907, a couple of men, named Parker and Reeder, traveling by horseback from San Francisco to Portland camped on the shores of the lake. The next morning they borrowed a skiff from Mrs. Mary Wittman, mother of the doomed Curly and widow of a homesteader, and took several soundings of the lake. The average depth was thirty feet, sufficient to make the lake an ideal fresh-water port, they explained.

Mrs. Wittman and other homesteaders around the lake were called together. With their help, Parker and Reeder asserted, the largest seaport between Seattle and San Francisco could be built on this site. A fortune was to be made. The two men told of connections in Washington that would enable them to get the federal government to dig a canal through the bar. Ships the world over would head for this seaport for everyone knew that fresh water killed sea growth on the hulls of ocean-going vessels.

The homesteaders were impressed. Within a couple of weeks, they turned over deeds for hundreds of acres of land to Reeder and Parker and from them collected thousands of dollars worth of unsecured promissory notes. A city was platted, large enough to accommodate thirty thousand people. The plats and the articles of incorporation were filed in the county courthouse in Gold Beach. Reeder and Parker went on to Portland to arrange for the "preliminary engineering."

Within a few weeks, salesmen carrying beautifully drawn artist's conceptions were selling 25×100-foot lots at $500 each to buyers throughout the Midwest and the East. At first, the port was named Pacific City, then changed to Crittendon. In less than two years some four hundred families had arrived in the West's "newest and most beautiful community." Most were disappointed when they discovered a lot twenty-five feet wide is rather narrow on which to build a house. The promoters, however, had thoughtfully staggered the sale of the lots so that most of the newcomers were able to pick up an adjoining lot for an additional $400.

The community developed with incredible speed. By December of 1909, it was the site of the "fanciest hotel between Portland and San Francisco," and had a business section of eight paved square blocks. It had a newspaper, a bank, three churches, schools, and stores. A census showed more than two thousand persons living inside the city limits and approximately the same number just outside of the city's border, all eagerly awaiting the arrival of the federal engineers who would build the canal and really start the boom.

Sometime between January and March of the following year, the residents discovered they no longer were living in Crittendon. The town was renamed Lakeport. Speaking before a meeting of the original homesteaders in the area, Parker explained that another town named Crittendon had been discovered that he, as mayor, and Reeder, as treasurer, merely had corrected the situation while in Portland. "You have nothing to fear," he promised. "And as soon as the canal is built we will have an election."

Everything awaited the construction of the canal, but the months continued to pass with no action. The newspaper editor realized his responsibility to his community and he wrote an editorial highly critical of the government's inexcusable delay in getting the canal underway. He sent copies to the Congress and to the U.S. Army Engineer's Office in Portland.

Within a few days after the editorial, a group of apologetic

Army engineers arrived in Lakeport from Portland. They knew nothing about the proposed canal, they explained, adding that the orders probably were tied up in Washington red tape. They would, however, start the preliminary surveys. The town rejoiced and turned out its entire population to watch the engineers at work. Their joy was short-lived. In a matter of a few hours, surveyors learned enough to tell the citizenry a sad tale.

The bottom of the lake was higher than sea level. If a canal were dug across the bar, there would be no Floras Lake. It would drain into the sea, leaving behind only a few small ponds. A canal lock? Impossible because the intake of the lake was much too meager to compensate for the loss of water in a lock operation.

The furious residents went to call on Reeder and Parker who were living at the Lakeport Hotel. Both had checked out a few moments after the Army engineers had checked in; called to Portland on urgent business, they said. A group of Lakeportians followed them to the City of Roses, but neither Reeder nor Parker were ever seen again.

The town died quickly. Within two months, its total population was less than one hundred. By 1913, it had a population of three—the irascible Neff, a charter member of the Lakeport Boosters Club and president of its Chamber of Commerce; an embittered Wittman, who inherited a batch of worthless promissory notes instead of a homestead; and Murphey, a gentleman of the road who had found the abandoned hotel a domicile to his liking.

Lakeport, however, could not be buried. Even after the dispute between Wittman and Neff had reduced its total population to zero, the town still proved a bonanza to unscrupulous real estate promoters. In the following years, two California firms picked up Lakeport lots from the county's delinquent tax rolls and resold them for the same price originally asked by Reeder and Parker. Not long ago, a couple from southern California appeared at the Curry County offices in Gold Beach to ask directions to Lakeport. They wanted to find the lot they had inherited in Lakeport's "most exclusive residential area."

Curry County officials see nothing humorous in the situation. Several legitimate investors have indicated interest in developing the area as a resort and summer community, but title holders to the tiny oblongs of land are scattered from

Murphey, slipped out of town and never returned. Neff ap-
been discovered and that he, as mayor, and Reeder, as treasurer, merely had corrected the situation while in Portland.
one coast to the other. Taxes on each lot amount to less than
a dollar a year. When tax collectors send out final demand
notices, required by law, most absentee owners send back
checks for another ten-year tax payment. The prevailing sentiment is that land so close to the ocean and on a large lake
in a forest, certainly must be worth more than a dollar a
year.

The buildings in the community were torn down long ago
for lumber. The only evidences of the vanished city now are
the faint outlines of streets, caved-in cellars, and a few pieces
of asphalt. On what was once the outskirts of the town are a
few attractive summer homes, built by wealthy Californians
and Oregonians. The choice locations with combined sea and
lake frontage are still bare, for it is here the cracker-box sized
lots are located.

Decades will pass before Lakeport will receive a proper
burial.

10

Two Petit Trianons

The French have contributed their share to the mysterious West. There was a period, shortly after the fall of Napoleon II, when the San Francisco Bay Area attracted French aristocrats and members of the upper middle class in droves. They were generally a cohesive group who looked down upon the "crude peasants, many of whom have amassed fortunes, who presume that their money obliges them to be disdainful of proper etiquette," according to the opinion of one French *émigré*.

Signs of the French influence probably are most prevalent in the city of Marysville, California, more than 150 miles northeast of San Francisco. Although founded by a Prussian, who named it New Mecklenburg, it was "sold" to a Frenchman names Charles Covillaud who promptly renamed the community Ney's Bar in honor of the French Marshal Michel Ney. This soon was corrupted by the peasants to "Nyes Bar." Another French *émigré* named Claude Chana joined Covillaud and shortly thereafter the duo became a trio with the arrival in the community of Augustus Le Plongeon.

Le Plongeon was a surveyor. The three men decided to turn the sprawling community into a classic city. When Le Plongeon had finished his survey, the city of Ney's Bar contained a broad street twenty blocks long named the Champs Elysées. There was a Place de la Concorde and the other newly created streets were appropriately named after assorted French heroes and nostalgic memories. Then, because the residents still insisted on calling Ney a Nye, the city was renamed Marysville in honor of Covillaud's wife. When the survey was finished, Le Plongeon became bored and moved on to achieve archeological fame for his work in the ruins of Yucatan and Quintana Roos in Mexico.

Floods have washed away the streets of Marysville countless times since it was born, but the streets have been replaced always as they were surveyed by Le Plongeon. The Champs Elysées is now E Street, and the Place de la Concorde is Washington Square, but there still are streets such as Lafayette and Napoleon as a reminder of its French beginning.

However, there are the remnants of the two French monuments in northern California that have almost been forgotten by all, yet each is the focal point of a most puzzling story. Although several miles apart, both of these monuments were once vast estates and both were patterned after the famed Petit Trianon of Marie Antoinette. The cost of each ran into the millions. Both were built by French aristocrats, and both were built for women. One, according to the legend, was built for an empress; the other for an infanta. Today there is little physical evidence of either Petit Trianon replica, yet each retains its mantle of mystery.

Alexander Duval was a widower and a retired engineer who had made a fortune building railroads in Chile and Peru. When he arrived in California he was accompanied by a staff of servants, an eight-year-old daughter, and a maid and a governess who attended only to the wants of the young girl.

The daughter's first name is unknown. From the time of her arrival in San Francisco until her disappearance, she was referred to only as *La Infanta*. For a while, Duval, his daughter, and entourage lived in a large ornate mansion in San Francisco where he entertained other members of the French colony in a most lavish manner. Between his parties, he scouted almost all of California looking for a proper site for his permanent home, finally purchasing a huge tract of land between Olivina and Cresta Blanca.

An architect was brought from Paris to design the estate, and most of the labor was performed by scores of Indians brought in from San Juan Bautista. The gardens and landscaping were copied after the Petit Trianon, but the greathouse was more baronial in concept, built of brick, five stories high with a mansard roof.

Duval was a connoisseur of fine wines and his estate was located in the heart of the California wine country. As soon as the mansion was completed, he built a series of three enormous vat houses, each three stories high over a deep cellar, and when these were finished, there came to the estate three cellar masters, one for each winery. The wineries staggered the imagination of the other wine makers in the vicinity. There were rows upon rows of shiny puncheons, made of oak brought from the Limousin forests of France and bound in brass. From France also came the presses, the wine racks, even the thousands of bottles and labels that would be needed when the wine was ready for marketing. While this was going on, hundreds of acres of land were being planted with rootlings from Côte d'Or and the Médoc.

At the roadway, spanning the long drive leading to the mansion, was a high archway which proclaimed the estate was the *Château Bellevue,* but few in the area referred to it as such. In a variety of pronunciations, it was known as the Petit Trianon. Duval called it "his daughter's house," or "the Infanta's home." The mansion was a magnificent building. The walls were more than three feet thick and paneled with carved mahogany. Huge crystal candelabras hung from the ceilings and on the walls hung rare tapestries and paintings.

The Infanta had a wing of her own which included a library, a bedroom, and separate rooms for her maid and her governess. More spectacular was the area adjoining her wing which Duval called her "play farm." It was a complete Burgundian hamlet, including a belfried chapel, a small school, a dairy, a coach house in which Duval kept his racing horses, a large aviary with pheasants and Scotch partridge, and cottages for the permanent workers on the estate.

On a lower tier beneath this was found a large marble terrace. In the center of the terrace was a large pool and from the center of the pool gushed a tall fountain. Swans swam lazily in the water as peacocks stalked along the paths.

Another wing of the mansion was devoted entirely to storage. Massive crates from France arrived regularly and were stacked unopened in the storage wing. They contained silverware and linens and some items of furniture to await the heirs of the fourth and the fifth generations.

Few people ever saw the Infanta and those who did merely caught a passing glimpse as she swept past in a carriage. Occasionally guests from San Francisco arrived for a weekend, and she was allowed to mix with these and with the priests who came from the Mission San Jose. Never did the

Infanta mingle with the natives, with the possible exception of a carefully supervised stroll through the play farm where the employees were housed.

There was a change for the Infanta when she became sixteen. Duval went to Paris to obtain a tutor for his daughter. After a most careful search, he selected a man in his late thirties who was eminently qualified for the job. A former child prodigy, he gave up a professorship at the Sorbonne to return with Duval to the Château Bellevue to teach the Infanta the finer points of academic learning; to give the proper background in drama, literature, and philosophy. Her seventeenth birthday was celebrated by a coming-out party attended by most of the proper residents of the San Francisco French colony. Occasionally the Infanta would leave the estate, accompanied by her father or her governess. Her most constant companion was her tutor. Duval was well pleased with his choice for his daughter; she was rapidly acquiring the high polish of the French aristocrat. He regretted, however, her increasing disinterest in the estate, but apparently he dismissed this as a temporary attitude on her part.

Shortly before the Infanta reached her eighteenth birthday, Duval was called to San Francisco on an overnight business trip. When he returned the following evening, he was greeted by the tearful governess who told him that the Infanta had disappeared . . . and so had the tutor. The preceding afternoon the Infanta and her instructor had slipped away from the governess, taken a carriage from the stables and driven to a distant railroad station, where the horse and carriage were abandoned. Although her wardrobe filled many closets, the Infanta carried away only two suitcases. Likewise, the tutor also had traveled lightly. Most of his possessions were left behind in the suite that had been his home for two years.

Duval hunted frantically for his daughter and her presumptuous tutor. Detectives followed them to San Francisco, but no trace of the couple could be found from the time they debarked from the train. Duval turned from a lavish host into a bitter recluse and died shortly after the turn of the century, leaving no will.

For a while, attorneys who had handled his affairs managed the estate and renewed the search for the lost Infanta along with any other possible heirs. The search into Duval's past was fruitless. On many occasions he had mentioned that his fortune started by building railroads in Chile and Peru, but Chilean and Peruvian officials knew of no Alexander Duval prominent in railroad construction. There were memories of a Jean Pierre Duval who had lived briefly in Lima, a wealthy French exile described as dark and lean, in his midfifties, and who had disappeared from Lima shortly before Alexander Duval appeared in San Francisco. The description matched, but Jean Pierre had no daughter living with him in Lima, nor a wife.

Eventually, even Duval's estate could not afford the search into his past and the continuing drain through legal fees and disinterested management. An auction was held. Other wine growers bought the French wine and the oaken puncheons brought from France, the wine racks and the bottles. The unopened crates of linen, china, and glassware, that were to last for five generations, were delightedly carried home by bargain-hungry housewives. Art dealers from San Francisco took possession of the tapestries and paintings.

Not sold at the auction were the acres upon acres of the finest wine grapes, now spoiling, unpruned and borne to the ground, now all that was left of the multi-million-dollar estate. Then one of the attorneys heard that the Infanta was living in a New York tenement, abandoned by her former lover and practically penniless. He wrote a letter to the address he had been given asking her what she would like to have done with her acres of spoiled wine grapes. A few weeks later he received an unsigned telegram from St. Louis, Missouri. It said: "Turn the cows loose in it."

Only the ruins of the mansion remained, a stark skeleton in the center of a hayfield. If the Infanta had children, there quite possibly is a third generation by now, but it is unlikely that they know of the fine French linen and silverware and chinaware imported to be saved for them. Who were they really, the mysterious Alexander Duval and the young girl known only as the Infanta?

It seems most unlikely that Alexander Duval and Paulin Caperon did not know each other. They had too much in common. Both were French, men of extreme wealth and of mysterious background. Both built replicas of the Petit Trianon at almost the same time; one for an Infanta and the other, quite possibly for an empress. Each was approximately the same distance from San Francisco, but in different directions, and Caperon's endeavor was on a much grander scale than Duval's. It is easy to speculate that one was responsible for the arrival of the other; aristocratic derelicts cast off in the upheaval following the exile of Napoleon II.

The Petit Trianon of Paulin Caperon was built in the tiny town of Mayfield, California, a community that no longer exists and long ago was swallowed by the expanding campus of Stanford University in Palo Alto. Today, more remains of this grandiose project than of Duval's. There is a small bridge ludicrously spanning nothing in the middle of a meadow, broken pipes angling upwards from the earth, some untrimmed cypress, and the remnants of a once massive stone water tower. Adjacent to the campus are long hidden tunnels which Caperon built for some unknown reason to link his castle with outlying parts of the estate. Some of the outer buildings remain, but have long lost their identity with the mysterious Petit Trianon of Palo Alto. One is used presently as an administration building for Stanford's housing project for married students. Another building designed as a library for the estate is now used by the Art and Architecture Department. The name of the extinct town lingers on through a small street called Mayfield Avenue on the southern edge of the campus along which one must drive to reach the clusters of fraternity houses. Oddly, very few of the students are aware that a large portion of their campus was a part of the mysterious Petit Trianon of Mayfield, or of the legend that it was built for use as a secret residence of the Empress Eugénie de Montijo, widow of Napoleon II. On at least three separate occasions during a decade, she was in residence in her American hideaway, once posing as Caperon's governess under the name of Eugénie Clogenson and twice using the name of a close friend, Eugénie Chaverson. There is much that lends support to this legend.

In the early 1870's, when the body of Napoleon II lay in a temporary sarcophagus in England where the Empress Eugénie was in exile, there appeared in the town of Mayfield a man with a heavy French accent who identified himself as Peter Coutts and implied that he was one of the Couttses or British banking fame. For a few days he rode through the area on horseback, studying the terrain and its uncurious inhabitants. Then, quietly, he purchased the 1,400-acre Matadero Rancho. The transaction was in cash and the sales price was not divulged. The stranger then let it be known that he wanted someone in the area to oversee the building of the estate; that speed in construction took precedence over economy and that there must not be the slightest variation in the building of the estate from the plans he had in his possession.

The man selected for the task was a Lucas Greer, a somewhat dour engineer who a few years earlier had retired from his practice in San Francisco to run a small farm in Mayfield. In an extraordinarily short time, some reports say less than a week, Greer had hundreds of men swarming over the acreage, and there is evidence that Coutts placed considerable trust in his overseer. In a letter written by Greer to a friend in San Francisco, he refers to the strange Frenchman who disappeared for weeks at a time, but "leaves generous funds for the completion of his folly."

The acreage of the Matadero Rancho included a huge meadow that rose gradually on its southern extremity into a high ridge. The plans called for construction of the castle on top of the ridge where a view could be commanded of the entire estate. The construction of the castle was to consist of massive rock, and the building was to rise five stories. Although the castle was to be the dominant structure, the program outlined by Coutts called for it to be the last building to be constructed. The first building to go up was a huge L-shaped structure with enormous rooms, each lined with walls of redwood panels framing pastoral scenes on printed chintz. The floors were parquet, covered with Aubusson rugs. The luxurious furnishings, as in the case of Duval, were imported from France. The bedroom walls were hung with folds of pleated chintz. The stem of the ell contained the bedrooms and private rooms, all opening into a hall with numerous niches for statuary or plants. The other wing, which formed the base of the ell, contained only the huge living room, the dining room, and the kitchen.

The second building to be erected was a smaller two-story structure. The ground floor apparently was designed as an administrative office for the estate. The second story was lined from ceiling to floor with book shelves which soon were stocked "with a train load of volumes in a variety of languages."

At the same time these two buildings were under construction, scores of workmen labored in other parts of the estate. A series of barns were built adjacent to a large private race track. A tall stone tower housed a water tank. The base for the castle on the hill was laid out, and small ponds and lakes were dug at the foot of the hill. The largest of the lakes contained small islands which could be reached by tiny bridges linking them together. The plans called for a series of underground passages leading from the castle site to no logical point. One report states that these tunnels were built in a search to find water, but this explanation does not appear plausible, as the passages were horizontal.

When the barns were finished, large shipments of blooded horses and cattle arrived at the Mayfield railroad siding and were driven to the Petit Trianon. Except for the castle, the construction project and the landscaping were completed in less than a year, and when it reached this stage, the man known as Peter Coutts appeared in a black frocked coat, yellow-topped boots, and a high black hat. Swinging a gold-mounted cane, he strode through the grounds of the estate "leaving no leaf unturned in his scrutiny."

A sign had been prepared to be hung from the arch over the entrance to the grounds which named the estate *La Petit Trianon.* On his inspection tour, the Frenchman paused as he watched workmen carry it toward the gate, then presently he ordered them to destroy it. The estate was to be known as Ayreshire Farm, he said. This was the only change he made in the plans given to Greer.

The residents of Mayfield thought it a much more practical name because, despite the peculiar tunnels that had been built, there seemed no doubt that Monsieur Coutts had any plans other than to run the estate as a farm. Herds of blooded cattle grazed on the land. More than a score of spirited horses were stabled, and there could be no other logical purpose for this than breeding. Even after the project was completed, it would continue to be the largest industry in the town. Excluding the builders, the estate maintained a weekly payroll of $7,500 for some three hundred permanent workers.

After completing his inspection of the estate, Monsieur Coutts again disappeared, this time for almost two months. When he returned, he was accompanied by an invalided woman whom he identified as his wife, two children, and another woman he introduced as a Miss Eugénie Clogenson, the governess for his children. "But it does appear that the Frenchman is more the servant of his governess," Greer wrote to his friend in San Francisco.

Greer was not alone in this impression. Other residents of

the village, many of whom worked on the estate, commented on the imperious manners of the titian-haired governess who never was seen shepherding her charges. However, when Miss Clogenson disappeared from the estate some three months later, to be replaced by a more subservient French governess, the villagers readily understood why. The woman obviously had been unsuited for such work.

Coutts did not mingle with the villagers. He left the estate, sometimes for weeks, leaving the management of the farm to Greer. The wife and two children kept to themselves in the large home. When the Frenchman was on the grounds, however, there were occasional large parties, but, again as in the case of Duval, those who were invited invariably were French and were presumed to have come from the San Francisco French colony. A tutor arrived, also French, to attend to the education of the children, and the servants noticed that he referred to the landlord as Monsieur Caperon and to the invalided woman as Madame Caperon. It was noticed also that most of the mail brought to Ayreshire Farm was addressed to a Mr. Paulin Caperon. Then another strange incident occurred.

The titian-haired woman of regal manner, first introduced as Miss Eugénie Clogenson, returned to Mayfield, about two years after her first visit. On this occasion, however, she was known as Miss Eugénie Chaverson, and there was no masquerade as a governess. She was accompanied by two maids who spoke only French "and in this language only to each other." Miss Chaverson was given the largest bedroom in the house, a room from which all servants other than her own were barred. Upon her arrival, the parties ceased, and there were no visitors to the estate. Occasionally she was seen strolling through the gardens. Once, one of the landlord's daughters accidentally bumped into Miss Chaverson. The girl was seen to back away quickly, curtsey, then run for the house with her hand over her mouth.

The length of Miss Chaverson's stay this time is unknown. She arrived; then, after a period of time, she was gone. Coutts, or Caperon, who had not left the grounds while Eugénie was present, again resumed his trips, and once again, there was an occasional party.

Almost six years went by before the mysterious Eugénie Chaverson came back to Ayreshire Farm. This visit was her longest—almost a year. As before, the parties ceased. Coutts-

Caperon remained on the grounds, and visitors were dis-
couraged. Greer had several discussions with his landlord
over the construction of the castle, but he noticed that
Coutts-Caperon no longer displayed the urgency over completion of the project that he had indicated at its inception.
They would spread the plans out on the tables in the administration office and discuss them at length, sometimes making
minor changes, but start of work on the grandiose castle
always was delayed. It seemed that Coutts-Caperon realized
that this phase of the project would remain only a dream.

One evening, almost a year after Eugénie Chaverson had
been in residence, the head groom came to the kitchen of the
main house. It was on a weekend and Greer was absent. One
of the prize Arabian mares was having trouble foaling, and
the groom thought the matter sufficiently serious to be
brought to Coutts-Caperon's attention. The landlord, he was
told, was dining in one of the larger private rooms in the
stem of the ell. He had left definite orders that he was not to
be disturbed. Even the service was being conducted by Miss
Chaverson's personal maids, and the consensus of those in
the kitchen was that the news of the mare's difficulty could
be delayed until after the dinner hour. The worried groom
thought otherwise and went in search of one of the French
maids to carry his message. In his haste, he blundered into
the room where the dinner was in progress, then froze in
astonishment.

Seated at the head of the table was Eugénie Chaverson and
on her head was an enormous emerald and diamond tiara.
Gathered around the table, their faces reflecting an equal
amazement at the interruption, were Coutts-Caperon, his in-
valid wife, and two strangers. The groom presently came to
his senses, stammered out his story, then fled when Caperon
waved him away.

It is unknown whether or not the landlord came to the
stable to see his prized mare. It is known, however, that by
morning, the groom's strange experience was known by most
of the three hundred workers employed on the farm, and it
is a reasonable assumption that his story soon moved beyond
Mayfield and that probably it was responsible for the strange
events that occurred about two weeks later.

They started with the unexpected arrival at Ayreshire
Farm of a middle-aged man in formal attire who identified
himself to the butler as the French consul general of San

Francisco who had urgent business to conduct with Monsieur Paulin Caperon. The butler took the visitor's card to his master who presently appeared and escorted the visitor to one of the private rooms off the foyer. Almost immediately a violent argument broke out between the two men, their voices carrying loudly through the heavy door to the ears of the curious butler who remained in the foyer. The argument was in French, which the butler could not understand, and it raged for the better part of a quarter hour before Eugénie Chaverson came down the long hall and entered the foyer. For a long moment, she listened to the conversation, then motioned for the butler to open the door to the room.

With her entrance, the argument ceased abruptly. For perhaps a half hour, the three remained in the room. Then the door opened, and the French consul-general stiffly walked across the foyer and out of the mansion to his waiting carriage. As the butler turned from closing the door, he saw Eugénie Chaverson walking back down the hall toward her private suite. Coutts-Caperon stood in the doorway to the room where the meeting had taken place. For a long moment he stared stonily at the butler. Then he sighed and with an elaborate Gallic shrug ordered the butler to oversee the packing of all the personal effects of the family.

Two days later, Coutts-Caperon, his wife and two children, Eugénie Chaverson, and her two French maids boarded a train at the Mayfield station and departed for San Francisco. They never returned.

There appears to be no record of what happened in the ensuing months at Ayreshire Farm. Apparently the horses and cattle were sold, as well as the furniture in the mansion. There is a record, however, as to the disposition of the 1,400-acre estate. It was sold to Leland Stanford in 1890, and the deed transfer was signed in London, England, by a Mme. E. Chaverson.

Who was the mysterious Eugénie Chaverson?

There are many historical references to a woman of this name and most identify her as a close friend of the Empress Eugénie, the widow of Louis Napoleon. One source indicates that both had a mutual friend in an Angela Burdett Coutts. The name Coutts is synonymous with wealth in Great Britain. At one time, the Coutts family controlled most of it through their powerful banks. The Couttses mingled with royalty. In addition to her friendship with the Empress Eugénie, Angela

Coutts once was described by the late King Edward VII as "after Victoria, the most remarkable woman in the kingdom." Angela had a cousin named Peter Coutts who obviously did not speak English with a heavy French accent.

There was a man named Paulin Caperon, the editor and publisher of the Paris newspaper *La Liberté*. Caperon was a fervent supporter of Napoleon II and was known to be a close friend of Peter Coutts who maintained a residence in Switzerland. In the chaos following the revolution, Caperon, accompanied by his invalided wife and two children, escaped from France to Switzerland, using Peter Coutts' identity and passport for safe passage.

The Empress Eugénie traveled constantly after the death of her husband, up until her own death at ninety-five in 1920. She maintained residences in Chiselhurst, London; Arenenberg on Lake Constance; at Farnborough in England, Cap Martin in Southern France, and on board her yacht, the *Thistle*. Her biographers report that often she would disappear for long periods of time, and that she traveled incognito.

She had ties to the United States. Her maternal grandfather was William Kirkpatrick, a Scotsman by birth, but an American citizen who for many years served as United States Consul at Malaga, Spain, the Empress' native land. It was an American dentist, Dr. T. W. Evans, who saved her life during the revolution in France. Evans procured the horses to carry them to Deauville, bribed the innkeepers en route to hide her identity, and found the British yachtsman who smuggled the Empress and her lady-in-waiting out of France to safety in England.

There is still another coincidence. Some years after Paulin Caperon left Mayfield so hurriedly, he returned to France. At Evian les Bains, he built a magnificent castle called *Château de Martelet*. It is known that the Empress was as frequent a visitor to his castle as was he to her yacht. Caperon died in 1890 and was buried at Bordeaux, and it was very shortly after his death, that Mme. E. Chaverson signed the deed of transfer for Ayreshire Farm to Leland Stanford.

It would not be stretching the truth too much if someone posted a sign at Stanford over a room in a building now used by the Art and Architecture Department, a sign stating "Empress Eugénie Slept Here."

There is another room on the large Stanford University campus that is surrounded by an aura of mystery. Locked and bolted for decades, its contents were hidden by an embarrassed Board of Trustees who took this action to solve a most perplexing problem.

Leland Stanford, the founder of the university, had a brother named Thomas Wellington Stanford who was a speculator, a promoter as adept as Leland, and a devotee of the mystic. For many years, Thomas Stanford lived in Australia, using it as a headquarters for innumerable trips throughout the South Seas on his explorations. His travels had a definite purpose—to collect apports, idols, fetishes, bundles of woven sea grass, rats' entrails, and all of the various paraphernalia used by medicine men, spiritualists, mediums, and soothsayers, all of whom Thomas believed to be endowed with special gifts beyond the comprehension of the ordinary man. Any volume in any language dealing with the supernatural or the occult and of which he had knowledge became part of his library.

Thomas Stanford died of malaria, contracted on one of his expeditions to New Guinea. His entire collection of occult devices along with a few tons of spiritualistic literature were bequeathed to Stanford University. Because of the relationship of the donor to the founder, it was a bequest that the trustees felt could neither be turned down nor discarded after acceptance. As a temporary solution, the gift was stored in a room in one of the campus buildings.

A few years ago, the late writer Idwal Jones heard of the bequest, went to Palo Alto, and sought permission to see it. He had considerable difficulty in locating anyone who knew of the incident and its temporary solution, but eventually he located a Professor Coover of the Department of Psychology who was aware of it. The professor spent several hours searching for a key, then accompanied Jones to the "Occult Room" hidden away on a colonnade. The collection was still there, untouched, covered with dust. Writing on a small box, barely legible, labeled its contents as "prepared rat entrails." A small sheaf of sea grass lay withered on the floor. Crates of books were piled from floor to ceiling and in one corner was an assortment of weapons ranging from spears to tiny daggers.

Recently, one of the writers was on the Stanford campus and asked if it still was possible to see the room. Numerous telephone calls were made, and to one official the writer re-called Jones' comment over the difficulty in finding a key to the room.

"Oh no, it's a little more than that," the university official explained. "They know it's around somewhere, but this time they appear to have lost the room."

11

The Extraordinary Doña Tula

One of the continuing mysteries of the West has been its long affection for the most notorious females. When Julia Bulette, the first prostitute to go into business on her own in Virginia City, Nevada, was murdered on her silken bed, every male in the town marched behind her coffin to the grave. It is, perhaps, a hangover from the times when the males outnumbered the females in a ten-to-one ratio. The so-called gentle sex was a rare commodity and therefore needed to be treated gently. This cannot explain the adulation accorded by the males to such female thugs as Calamity Jane or Belle Starr, but it is an attitude that continues even today in the less urban areas of the West.

Prostitution, for example, still is legal in the State of Nevada, except in Las Vegas where gambling casino operators want no tourist wasting their time in a bordello when they could be losing their money on a dice table. Not long ago a ministerial alliance decided that prostitution must go in another Nevada city and were responsible, after a considerable effort, for having the proposal placed upon the ballot during a municipal election. When the returns were counted, one newspaper gleefully bannered the results in this manner:

MINISTERS LOSE WHORE WAR IN WINNEMUCCA

It was almost axiomatic that the more perfidious the female, the greater the adulation. Very rarely did public indignation ever rise against the gentler sex. Once, in a small town in Montana, a young woman and her lover were hung on the outskirts of the community after they had murdered a couple of passing strangers. Another traveler, who arrived on the scene a short time later, cut down the woman and brought her into town and had no trouble in securing "a good Christian burial" for the lass. Her lover was left hanging on the tree.

Verona Baldwin drilled her cousin, multimillionaire Lucky Baldwin, with a few well-placed bullets. Lucky Baldwin survived to find public opinion against him so strong that the only manner in which he could quiet it was to pay off Verona. She used the money to open a lush brothel in Denver.

From Austin, Nevada, to San Francisco, there are theaters named after the Swedish nightingale Jenny Lind and oldtimers still will tell of the crowds that Jenny attracted when she sang in the West. They refuse to believe that Jenny, brought to this country by P. T. Barnum, never traveled west of Chicago. Books have been written about courtesans ranging from Lola Montez to Sally Stanford, yet oddly, very little ever has been told about a beautiful young woman named Gertrudes Barcelo, one of the most mysterious and perfidious wenches ever known in the West. A fecund young woman of incredible beauty, she had the soul of a witch whose victims went happily to their ruin for the privilege of her continued favor.

Her origins are obscure. Some say she came from the small town of Taos, New Mexico; others contend she was born in Barcelona, Spain, and brought to the New World by her lover, a Spanish lieutenant, when she was a child of fourteen.

She was in her mid-teens when she first appeared in Santa Fe, the City of the Holy Faith, in 1820, in the company of a Spanish officer named Luis Corzo Velázquez. What happened to Velázquez is not clear, but shortly after her arrival, Gertrudes became the mistress of a man named Gonsálvez who operated a small gambling hall on el Calle de San Francisco in Santa Fe; within a very short time after this affair, Gonsálvez disappeared, leaving Gertrudes Barcelo in the possession of a large amount of money and the sole proprietor of the gaming hall which she named *Las Tulas*. It was a name that became synonymous with her own and one that she used for the rest of her life.

It was incongruous that a woman of Doña Tula's age could

at this time operate her own business in a Spanish outpost city, yet she prospered almost at once. From a small gambling house patronized by soldiers, *Las Tulas* expanded into the most elaborate and elegant rendezvous in the gay capital. The soldiers were made unwelcome and were replaced by the leading political figures and merchants of the territory.

The most elaborate furnishings were brought overland to Santa Fe from the distant United States, including magnificent pier glass mirrors, deep-napped carpets, and crystal chandeliers. It offered the finest cuisine to be had outside of Mexico City, served in private rooms attended by the most beautiful prostitutes to be found in New Spain. Periodically, elaborate *bailes* were arranged at *Las Tulas* and sometimes, if a guest was of sufficient prominence, the beautiful Doña Tula would attend to all of his wants personally.

Eventually, these personal attentions from Doña Tula ceased when she became the envied mistress of the most powerful man in New Mexico, none other than the governor, Don Manuel Armija. Don Manuel made no secret of his infatuation, so great indeed, that Doña Tula soon was given her private quarters in the governmental palace. The daring liaison, which Don Manuel made no attempt to keep secret, brought her into contact with all the figures of government, and what gossip and information she could not learn from them, she easily wheedled from Don Manuel as they lay in their bed.

Most governmental functions, affairs of state, and entertainment of almost all dignitaries were conducted at *Las Tulas,* and the cost of the expensive parties was borne by the distant government in Mexico City. A steady flow of money ran from the treasury to the vaults of Doña Tula, yet it still could not satisfy the calculating raven-haired beauty. Or perhaps she was hedging her bets, in the manner of the professional gambler that she was, for the secrets she gleaned from the bed of Don Manuel were rapidly being fed back to the United States government and most certainly for a fee.

When the army of General Stephen W. Kearny approached Santa Fe, it was Doña Tula who convinced Don Manuel he should flee and avoid battle. At the same time, because of her great love, she would remain behind temporarily until she could get word to Don Manuel as to the best psychological time for him to return with his army and slaughter the unprepared Americans. Thus, when General Kearny entered the historic city, there was not the slightest opposition. Don Manuel had disappeared with his entire garrison.

The only outward change in Doña Tula's habits was that she no longer maintained quarters beside her lover in the governmental palace. The casino prospered under the American occupation even more than it had under the Don Manuel regime. Officers from the United States now were wined and entertained in the private rooms, and it was their money that disappeared at the monte tables rather than that of the Mexicans. General Kearny raised no objection. After all, it was because of Doña Tula that his army had taken Santa Fe without a casualty, and in addition, this beautiful creature still kept him informed of the plans of Don Manuel Armija. Had it not been for her, the occupation authorities would not have learned that Armija's agents had drifted back into the city and were planning a surprise attack upon the garrison.

Don Manuel meanwhile, was exceptionally proud of his mistress. She was behaving like a general, calling for key men of the former Mexican garrison to be infiltrated into the City of the Holy Faith. She provided them with safe quarters and false identities. At the same time she took care of the finances for the pending revolt, taking contributions not only from the absent Don Manuel but also from leading citizens of Santa Fe who chafed under the military rule of the United States Army. Secret meetings even were held in *Las Tulas* by those planning the rebellion, and they marveled at her audacity in plotting the coup directly over the heads of the American officers who wenched, wined, and gabled below.

The key members of the revolt inspired by Doña Tula were Colonel Don Diego Archuleta, the Reverend Juan Felipe Ortiz, and a Tomás Ortiz, whose relationship to the priest, if any, is unknown. Word was sent to Don Manuel that the revolt would occur on Christmas Eve, and that as soon as the garrison was seized, Don Manuel was to return with his army. Men were detailed to spike the artillery on the plaza. The recently appointed governor, Charles Bent, was to be seized in the palace, where he had taken over Don Manuel's quarters, and the commanding officer, Colonel Sterling Price, also was to be captured in his home. The time for the uprising was set for eleven in the evening, and, in the spirit of Hidalgo, was to be triggered by the sounding of the church bells.

A little less than two hours before the appointed hour,

Doña Tula urgently summoned Don Diego and Tomás Ortiz to her casino. Something had gone wrong, she said in great agitation. She had first noticed that the number of the occupation officers in the casino was exceedingly sparse for a holiday evening. She then had enticed an officer into telling her that most of the men were on duty because an uprising was expected that evening, but that the ringleaders were known and were to be arrested just before the revolt was scheduled. Don Diego and Tomás must flee for their lives. The revolt must wait for a more propitious moment. Doña Tula had no idea who had betrayed them, but she would find out and let them know. Meanwhile, the two men must escape on the horses she had arranged to be waiting for them.

Don Diego and Tomás galloped out of the city, most grateful to the passionate Doña Tula for her warning. The information she conveyed to them was absolutely correct. A quarter hour before the bells pealed from the church, United States soldiers entered a score of houses within the city and quickly arrested the other leaders in the conspiracy. The insurgents were picked up as they converged on the plaza, and when Father Juan rang out his bells, he was rewarded only by the laughter of the occupation soldiers outside of the church.

Father Juan was not arrested, possibly out of fear that his jailing would trigger another uprising in the City of the Holy Faith. When Christmas arrived at midnight, the casino of *Las Tulas* was the height of revelry and the celebrants were all officers of the occupation troops. There are some who say that as the party progressed Doña Tula took Colonel Sterling Price by the hand and led him upstairs to one of the private rooms where they spent the remainder of the night.

Don Diego and Don Manuel never returned to Santa Fe. About a month after the former's flight, according to the legend, "a Mexican of aristocratic mien" entered the casino and for several hours waited quietly at a bar until Doña Tula put in an appearance. She paled as she saw him, and ran toward the stairs with the Mexican in swift pursuit. She screamed. A shot was fired, and the Mexican fell to the carpets, dead. There is no record of who he was or who shot him.

The casino prospered as it never had before. As Santa Fe slowly turned from an occupied city into an American garrison where the officers brought their wives, there were a few complaints about her operations. The wives were upset over the flamboyant bordello and gambling den, but to no avail. They succeeded only in arousing the animosity of Doña Tula. She demanded and was granted access to the social affairs conducted by the army and members of the territorial government. The diary of Mrs. Susan Magoffin, the wife of an influential and rich merchant, tells of one of the exclusive and social balls given by the garrison in the city.

"There was Doña Tula, the principal monte bank keeper of Santa Fe," she wrote, "a stately dame of a certain age, the possessor of a portion of that shrewd sense and fascinating manner necessary to allure the wayward, inexperienced youth to the hall of final ruin."

Not all were wayward and inexperienced. The lushly furnished rooms above the casino that once catered to the whims of the Mexican aristocracy now were patronized by their equivalents visiting from the nation's capital and the civic and military leaders of the community. The rooms still were attended by the youngest and most beautiful prostitutes to be found in the Southwest, and they were thoroughly trained in their art. Doña Tula became known as one of the richest women in the Southwest.

As she grew older and her body changed from that of the voluptuous courtesan to that of a fleshy dowager, her personality became irascible and arrogant. The high cheek bones that had contributed to her incredible beauty as a young woman now gave her a rapacious look. Younger newcomers to the city wondered why such an ill-tempered woman who ran a whorehouse and a gambling joint still was invited to all of the social functions of the city and more, also wondered why she would attend. Then, after a few months in the city, they sensed that she was feared and it was from this fear that she derived her power. The reason for the fear could only be conjectured, but one possible answer was that it came about from many hundreds of secrets Doña Tula had acquired from the many patrons of her lush sexual gymnasium above the casino.

Doña Tula died suddenly in her elaborate home near the casino in 1851. There are some who believe her death was as mysterious as her origin, but there is no record as to whether she was murdered or died from natural causes. Within moments of her death, however, a detachment of soldiers appeared in the casino of *Las Tulas*. The most beautiful and accomplished whores in the Southwest were ordered to pack up and leave behind the customers. The soldiers then conducted a most methodical search of the premises. The carpets were lifted, the gambling tables, the furniture, and even the beds were carefully taken apart. Paper was peeled from the walls, and the boards were raised from the floors. Not known is the object of such a painstaking search nor whether or not the search was successful.

There was one man who had never succumbed to Doña Tula's wiles, nor apparently had he ever forgiven her for her obvious doublecross of Don Manuel and Don Diego. This was the priest who had rung the bells to trigger the abortive coup. No longer was he a mere priest. Now he was the Right Reverend Juan Felipe Ortiz, the Bishop of Santa Fe. He achieved his revenge against Doña Tula in a manner that would turn a present-day Los Angeles mortician green with envy.

The bishop took charge of the funeral arrangements and ordered a most expensive funeral. For the services in the church there was a fee of $5,000, plus the fees of the bishop, which came to another $1,000. There was an additional expense for *los pasos,* a $500 charge for each time the funeral procession halted on its way to the burial ground from the church when the bier was placed on the ground. The cost of the spiritual services at the graveside before interment cost another $1,600. In addition to all of this were fees for miscellaneous expenses which matched the set charges. It was enough to make the miserly Doña Tula turn over in her grave.

What happened to the remainder of her estate, if any, is as much a mystery as are her birth and her death. She left no legacy. The interior of her casino and house of pleasure was ripped apart moments after her death. The shell of the building has long since lost its identity and there is disagreement in Santa Fe as to its precise location. If a headstone still marks her grave, it has been forgotten.

If she had died young, a victim of an assassin's bullet or even the hangman's noose, she would have been remembered as a beautiful, if treacherous, woman and would have been better known than any Calamity Jane or Belle Starr. But she suffered the worst fate that can befall any woman who wins fame or power or fortune through her beauty. She lived too long. The image she left at the time of her death was that of a vicious witch rather than a beautiful courtesan and these memories inspire neither romantic biographies nor historical plaques. It is unfortunate, because she was one of the most extraordinary women of the mysterious West.

12

Will the Real Mark Hopkins?

There are few people in this country to whom the name of Mark Hopkins is unfamiliar. In San Francisco, the Hotel Mark Hopkins still presides majestically over the city from Nob Hill, built on the spot that Mark Hopkins chose for the site of his many cupolaed mansion more than a century ago. To many in the United States, it is this hotel that has made the name famous. Scholars and theologians, however, may bring to mind the educator and clergyman of the last century, who bore the same name, but who was not related to the West.

To the westerner, and particularly the Californian who has been resident long enough to acquire some knowledge of the history of the state, the name is identified with those of Leland Stanford, Collis Huntington, and Charles Crocker; members of the Big Four who started their careers as merchant cronies in Sacramento during the Gold Rush and rose to become the most powerful and wealthy men in the West. The story of their success and the events that caused it has been well covered by historians. The lives of Huntington, Crocker, and Stanford have been explored in detail, yet in no standard encyclopedia of America's prominent men is there a biography of Mark Hopkins, the other member of the Big Four. He moves like a wraith through the history of the mysterious West.

As Hopkins' position in life changed from that of a small hardware merchant to that of a railroad tycoon, he brought two other men bearing his same name into close business and personal contact with him, one of whom mysteriously disappeared. When the magnate died in his private railroad car in Yuma, Arizona, the obituary writers were as confused as to which was the *real* Mark Hopkins as are most Californians today.

In the Sacramento City Cemetery there is a large mausoleum bearing the name of Mark Hopkins. In it lies the bodies of Mark Hopkins, the railroad magnate, and three other Hopkinses; Moses and Ezra Augustus, identified by tht inscription as brothers of Mark, and Samuel, described as their nephew. The mausoleum, bordered by date palms and urns, was built by a Mary Sherwood Hopkins, who is as much of an enigma as the Mark inside the tomb. Records show that she was married to the Mark Hopkins who disappeared, later became the mistress of Moses, and when Moses married, became the house companion of Mark, the magnate. When the latter Mark died, she assumed the role of his wife and inherited as her share of the estate some $70 million.

Mary moved back to her native Massachusetts where she built a $2.5 million home in the Berkshires. When she was seventy-three, she contracted with Herter & Company of New York for a new interior for her dolomite castle. The company sent up a decorator named Edward F. Searles, then about forty-six, whom Mary promptly married. When she died a few years later, she left the entire estate to Searles, a matter which considerably upset her only adopted son, Timothy Nolan Hopkins. He contested the will. While the matter was pending a court hearing in Salem, Massachusetts, Timothy bitterly dropped a few hints as to the manner in which his adopted mother had obtained the fortune.

The case was settled before it reached the court when Timothy accepted $12 million from Searles. But there had been sufficient publicity over the matter to alert a host of Hopkinses in South Carolina that they probably were the "rightful heirs" to the vast Mark Hopkins fortune.

At this writing, a luncheon meeting is held every Wednesday in a small San Francisco restaurant by representatives of these "rightful heirs" to discuss the progress of their endeavors to recover what they believe to be their inheritance. The group is headed by a Mrs. Estelle Cothran Latta who claims descendancy from Mark Hopkins on both her father's and mother's side. She estimates the estate has appreciated into the billions during the past century, and that in the interests of justice it should be retrieved and redistributed. She has been enjoined by the Securities and Exchange Commission from selling any more stock to the "rightful heirs" to finance the battle, but her efforts have intrigued many lawyers who have studied the results of her research.

It is Mrs. Latta's contention that only a small fraction of the estate was diverted from the "rightful heirs" into the purse of the amorous widow and to the account of her former lover, Moses, and that this was a necessary payoff to insure their silence on a conspiracy by the three survivors of the Big Four. The major portion of the Mark Hopkins fortune, which included banks, railroads, steamship lines, transit lines, and even whole city blocks, wound up in the possession of Huntington, Crocker, and Stanford.

As he became more prominent, Mark Hopkins deliberately attempted to obscure his past, and it was with this in mind that he became closely associated with two other men of the same name and thus assumed a protective camouflage by gradually adopting their background as his own. There are some who contend that the idea of three Mark Hopkinses is a myth, but there are enough records and documentation still in existence to prove that there were indeed Mark Hopkinses three. There also is sufficient documentation still available to show that only one of the men buried with the railroad tycoon is his brother, and that the other two bear no relationship to him at all.

The Mark Hopkins who became the rail tycoon was born in Richmond County, Virginia, and when a young boy, he moved with his family to Pearson County in North Carolina. The Hopkins family later drifted into Orange County and then Randolph County, settling in New Hope Township. Mark was one of twelve children born to Hannah Crow and Net Hopkins. Of the dozen, the only two that are pertinent to later developments in the West are Mark, who was born in 1814, and his younger brother Moses, who was born three years later.

Moses, in the idiom of today, probably would be described as a swinger. A century ago he was identified as a youth of weak moral fiber. He gambled and swore and drank to excess and upended many a lass in a haystack. One young maiden insisted on marriage, and he obliged, moving with her temporarily to the adjacent Orange County. The bliss soon became boredom, and he left her. She returned to her parents. Moses immediately hoisted the skirts of another fecund young lady and soon thereafter married her to protect her fair name. He forgot however to divorce his first wife and presently found himself facing charges of bigamy, nonsupport, and desertion.

He was released under bail, then was rearrested on a series of petty larceny charges, and again released under bail to await trial. He then promptly committed a more serious crime, the conviction of which could result in his execution. He stole a horse.

Records in the Orange County Courthouse at Hillsboro, North Carolina, show that he was brought to trial on September 12, 1845, on a count of grand larceny involving the theft of a mare. The records show also that Moses asked for a postponement in the proceedings. One of the affidavits signed by Moses in connection with this request is, according to handwriting experts, identical to the signature of Moses on existing documents in California, thus establishing that the two men were the same.

The request for continuance was denied. Moses was found guilty, sentenced to thirty-nine lashes at the public whipping post, sixty days in jail, plus another thirty-nine lashes immediately prior to his release from jail, plus costs. He escaped the death sentence because, according to the records, "he prays for himself the benefit of clergy." The clerical loophole apparently would work only once. If he was convicted of stealing another horse, there was nothing that could save him from a public hanging.

Moses and Mark apparently were closer to each other than to the other members of the large family, and because of this close fraternal friendship, Moses never served his full sentence. Nor did he ever stand trial for bigamy and petty larceny. Mark waited long enough for the wounds from the first lashing to heal. Then, in a coup more germane to the West than to North Carolina, he broke into the jail, forced the turnkey at gunpoint to release Moses, then take his place in the cell. By dawn, the two Hopkins brothers were miles away.

Apparently there was no hue and cry, and the brothers must have understood that there would be none. At that time, many of the Southern states, as some of the Western states do still, maintained a "good riddance" attitude. Today, for example, the State of New Mexico has a "conditional release" system for first offenders or discharged prisoners. The condition is that the prisoners must leave the state and never come back, and it saves the New Mexican taxpayer untold millions in probationary expenses and recurrent crimes.

The two Hopkins brothers made no attempt to change their identity. However, their movements and whereabouts during the next few years are sketchy. One account places them on a Kentucky farm owned by relatives. Another has the pair operating a hardware store in New Orleans. But no one seems to know their movements for certain.

On May 24, 1851, however, the *Daily Alta* of San Francisco listed some 250 passengers arriving in the city on board the steamship *Columbus* in from Panama. Two of these passengers were a Mark and Moses Hopkins of North Carolina.

One year and two days before Mark Hopkins was born in Virginia, another Mark Hopkins was born in the town of Henderson, New York, a small community on the northeastern shores of Lake Ontario. Oddly, he was the grandson of a Moses Hopkins who operated a small general store in Great Barrington, Massachusetts. This Mark was one of eight children, one of whom was a brother named Ezra Augustus. None of the children were named after their grandfather. The father ran a small merchandise store.

In 1825, this Hopkins family drifted toward the west, living for a while in Buffalo, New York, then finally settling in St. Clair, Michigan, where the senior Hopkins, who also was named Mark, became a solid burgher. Here he ran a general merchandise store, became the community's first probate judge and postmaster. When he died suddenly in 1828, Mark, Jr., dropped out of high school, and for at least two years he worked in the family store. He then moved to Lockport, New York, where he opened up a general store with a partner named Hughes. This was not a successful venture apparently, for a short time later he entered into another partnership with a man named Williams, this time selling farm supplies.

This business also failed to prosper. He returned to St. Clair, again worked in the family store, then once again went back to Lockport. This time he was accompanied by his brother, Henry, an attorney, and for a while Mark studied law under his tutelage. Henry died. Mark abandoned the idea of becoming a lawyer and moved to New York City where he became a bookkeeper with the firm of James Rowland & Co.

When news of California's gold strike at Sutter's Creek

reached New York, Mark Hopkins felt the compulsion to head West. He quit his job, formed the New England Mining Company, raised $13,000 to buy mining equipment, and sailed with his stock, his brother, Ezra Augustus, and a friend aboard the steamship *Pacific* for the long journey around the Cape. The vessel departed from New York on January 22, 1849.

Through a note of thanks to the captain of the ship, printed in the *Daily Alta*, the arrival of the New York Mark Hopkins in San Francisco is set on August 10, 1849, almost two years prior to the arrival of Mark and Moses of North Carolina.

The New York Mark and Ezra Augustus left immediately for Sacramento to open a store. This city was the merchandising center of the spread-out mining towns of the Mother Lode Country of California. The demand for nearly everything far exceeded the supply, and almost all of the gold the miners panned from the earth was plucked from their pockets by the merchants. Eggs sold for a dollar each; a loaf of bread brought four dollars. A shovel purchased in New York for fifty cents could bring as much as fifty dollars from a desperate miner.

The two New York Hopkinses sold all of their stock in about a week, then disbanded the New England Mining Company. Much of their profit was invested in real estate, one of the few items that could be purchased in the city at a comparatively inexpensive price. Mark went into a partnership with an Edward Miller to open a grocery store. Ezra Augustus homesteaded a large farm in Solano County, apparently to raise the produce that his brother was to sell. By the time Moses and his brother appeared on the California scene, the two New York Hopkinses were quite wealthy and well established in the bourgeoning Sacramento community.

The North Carolina Mark and Moses did not linger in San Francisco. They went directly to Hangtown, since renamed Placerville, and staked out a claim, but it proved barren. Possibly taking the idea from his namesake in Sacramento, the southern Mark decided to go into the grocery business in Hangtown. For some, it was a good community from a business point of view. Philip D. Armour started his meat-packing empire there with a small butcher shop. John Studebaker, a name long familiar with transportation, also began in Hangtown, where he made wheelbarrows for the miners. The southern Mark, however, did not do well in Hangtown. It was during this time that the four Hopkinses became friendly, and that their backgrounds began to blend. It started perhaps, when Moses left Hangtown and went to work as a clerk in the Sacramento grocery store operated by the northern Mark. A short time later, the northern Mark bought out his partner. The southern Mark folded his Hangtown grocery store, moved to Sacramento, and went into the retail hardware business. Thus, early in 1854, in Sacramento, one Mark Hopkins was operating a large grocery store and less than a block distant, another Mark Hopkins was running a hardware store.

In the evening of July 13, 1854, a fire started in a paint storeroom of the Sacramento Hotel, and before the volunteer fire department could control it a half block of the city was destroyed, including the hardware store of the southern Mark. Another victim of the same blaze was Collis P. Huntington, who also operated a hardware store. When they rebuilt, they went into partnership, forming the first half of what later was to be known as the Big Four.

At the time of the fire, the northern Mark was gone. He had closed his store temporarily while he returned to New York to marry his cousin, Mary Frances Sherwood, a native of Great Barrington, Massachusetts. She is possibly the greatest enigma of the "affaire Hopkins." The descriptions of her vary. A boardinghouse keeper where she once remained for a week described her as a woman of "beautiful figure with long black hair bound over a rat and with cold blue eyes that always looked through you as if you were not present." Newspaper accounts refer to her as "gay" and "charming" and "stately."

Mary Sherwood is believed to be the daughter of Lydia and William Sherwood, and the construction of her castle in the Berkshires of Massachusetts indicate that she did have ties to Great Barrington. According to her marriage certificate, she was thirty-six years old when she married the northern Mark Hopkins on September 29, 1854, and she was a spinster at the time. The same certificate, however, also identified her as Ellen Sherwood. The New York *Herald*, of September 22, 1854, mentioned the marriage between Mary Sherwood and Mark Hopkins of Sacramento City, California. The minister who performed the ceremony omitted the bride's first name on two occasions where it could have been mentioned in the records of the church.

The most significant item about the New York records pertaining to the marriage is that they were signed by the northern Mark. Five days later, the southern Mark signed homesteading papers before a notary in the United States Land Office in San Francisco. In those days obviously it was impossible to travel from one coast to the other within such a short time, and this is another point against the contentions of those who assert that there was only one Mark Hopkins. The homestead was the one adjacent to the farm of Ezra Augustus and was the one operated by Moses.

The northern Mark returned to California with his bride. They bought three adjoining lots in one of the most fashionable sections of the city, each signing the deed in compliance with California's community property laws, and built a large home. A short time later, they invited the nephew of the northern Mark to come from St. Clair and live with them until he became established. His name also was Mark Hopkins, adding to the confusion. They had no children, but later adopted an orphan named Timothy Nolan.

Both the earlier Mark Hopkinses prospered. The southern Mark, with Huntington, gradually expanded their store into one of the largest importing firms in the West. The northern Mark not only did well in his store, but also speculated successfully in real estate.

Friends and acquaintances differentiated among the three men by calling the southern member of the trio "Big Mark," the northern member "Little Mark," and the nephew "Young Mark." The records of the city, however, were not so discriminating. In the spring of 1855, a Mark Hopkins was elected to the Sacramento City Council, and no one knows which of the three it was. Some historians assume it was the southern Mark and that it was here he met Leland Stanford, a drygoods dealer, and Charles Crocker, another merchant, who later combined to form the Big Four.

It was about this time that there came to Sacramento a young man named Theodore Dehone Judah, a twenty-seven-year-old engineer who had built bridges and helped plan the construction of the Niagara Gorge Railroad. It was Judah who waved the wand that transformed four Sacramento merchants into railroad tycoons of incredible wealth.

Judah was brought to Sacramento by a group of businessmen who wanted a short railroad built from the city to the Hangtown mines. Judah surveyed the most practical route, and the line was built. The last spike had barely been driven, however, before the Hangtown mines were down to their last few ounces of gold. The railroad became useless as Hangtown rapidly dwindled into the Placerville it is today.

Judah was obsessed with the idea of railroads, and his greatest dream was to promote and participate in the construction of a transcontinental line. He was not alone in this dream, but he surely was the youngest, the most poorly financed, and the least likely to be given serious consideration for participation in such a project.

For some time, the manner of financing railroads in the West, and in Texas particularly, had followed a pattern. Railroads were considered as necessary to the development of a community as were bridges and roads. Towns needed railroads to ensure future growth, but in many of these communities the individuals who could afford to help finance rail construction were reluctant to do so. Railroad promoters overcame this problem by a form of "switch financing."

Small political entities, such as towns, cities, or counties, would issue bonds which would then be exchanged for railroad stocks or bonds. The municipal bonds, or their equivalent, then were sold at large discounts to eastern banks or investors who had refused to invest in railroad stocks.

As could be expected, eastern investors eventually became chary of municipal bonds from small western cities and the railroads turned to the federal government for help. By mid-century, the practice of federal aid to railroads in the form of extensive land grants was firmly established. Railroad companies were given alternate sections of the public domain within a six-to-ten-mile radius on either side of the proposed line. The railroad then sold the land to investors and settlers who speculated that a rail line near their property would result in an increased land value. It has been estimated that the federal government gave away some 180 million acres of land with a value of nearly a billion dollars.

Judah first surveyed a practical route for a rail line through the precipitous Sierra Nevada Range, a route still used today by the Southern Pacific Railroad. He next journeyed to Washington and won some tentative commitments for help in his project from the Congress. Upon his return to California, he persuaded several citizens in the tiny community of Dutch Flat to put up almost $50,000 to help meet the organizational costs of his Central Pacific Railroad. He next went to San

Francisco in an attempt to obtain matching funds, but the bankers were in no manner receptive to his plan. He turned to Sacramento. Here, in a small room above the store of Huntington and Hopkins, he won his financing and lost his railroad.

Present at this meeting, in addition to the southern Mark and Huntington, were Leland Stanford, the Sacramento wholesale grocer, and Charles Crocker, a drygoods dealer. The four men, the Big Four, that night agreed to incorporate the Central Pacific Railroad. Capital was set at $8.5 million, to be raised by the sale of hundred dollar shares. Each member of the quartet subscribed to 150 shares and elected himself, along with Judah and three others, as the directors.

Judah made a more detailed survey of his route in the western end of the proposed railroad, then once again made the lengthy trip to the nation's capital. His timing could not have been better. The Civil War was underway, and Congress was most receptive to any plan that would tie the West more closely to the North. Two Pacific Railroad acts were passed within a two-year period. The Central Pacific Railroad was authorized to build a rail line to the East, continuing until it met up with the Union Pacific which at the same time was authorized to extend its lines westward. At the same time, the Central Pacific was given approval to build its lines west to San Francisco and south from both San Francisco and Sacramento.

A four-hundred-foot right-of-way was granted for the construction of the lines and stations, and in addition the promoters were granted the ten alternate sections per mile on both sides of the line for the entire length of the railroad. On top of this, the generous Congress loaned the railroad enough cash to build the line which, in some areas, amounted to $48,000 per mile.

The Big Four held a rigid, unbreakable control over the corporation as well as the many subsidiary corporations that were formed as a result of the railroad. They organized a construction company to build the railroad and a bank to handle the money that was pouring in from the government and from the sale of the land grants. So secret were their transactions and so limited was their bookkeeping that to this date no one ever has been able to determine how much of the United States Treasury wound up in the possession of the Big Four. The few ledgers that were maintained "accident-

ally" were destroyed in a fire shortly after the government
announced plans to investigate the entire affair.

Long before this, however, the northern Mark had turned
the operation of his store over to others and joined the Central Pacific Railroad as the corporation treasurer. The Michigan Mark Hopkins was named deputy treasurer.

Meanwhile, Mary Frances Sherwood Hopkins was spending more and more time in Solano County at the prosperous
farm of her brother-in-law, Ezra Augustus. Sometimes the
visits would extend for months, usually during the summer
and fall when the weather was so warm in Sacramento. Ezra
and Moses remained good friends. On January 2, 1863, the
two men went to the U.S. Land Commission Office in San
Joaquin County where Ezra completed the final papers to
acquire the deed to his homestead. Moses made out an affidavit in which he stated he had known Ezra for about ten
years and that Ezra had lived on the land since 1854. Ezra
died about two years later. Thirteen years later, after the
death of the southern Mark, Ezra's body was disinterred and
placed in the Sacramento mausoleum that Mary built and
where the inscription identifies him as the brother of Moses,
the man who had known him for about ten years.

Not long after Ezra's death, the northern Mark Hopkins
vanished. The disappearance was not a spectacular one. Although he was treasurer of a large railroad, a highly successful businessman, and one of the leading merchants in the
State Capital of California, he simply vanished. These writers
have combed newspapers of the era and can find no obituary
notice nor any reference to an illness or death. There was a
family plot in a St. Clair cemetery, but his body is not there
unless the grave is unmarked. His disappearance caused no
more comment than would that of a vagrant leaving a strange
city. What happened to his real estate holdings? His money?
His estate? No one seems to know. What happened to his
wife and his adopted son, Timothy? There is no mystery here.
They moved in with Moses Hopkins on his farm in Solano.

It was not a platonic friendship. Years later when Timothy
sued his adopted mother's last husband, he testified that Mary
Sherwood Hopkins and Moses were lovers, but that the romance cooled after they had lived together a while. The
length of time that Mary and Moses lived together is unknown. Timothy testified that Moses deserted her to marry

another woman, apparently forgetting the two wives he had left behind in North Carolina.

Desertion is probably too strong a word. It is more likely that the romance cooled, that they parted on friendly terms, for Timothy testified also that Moses was responsible for moving her into the home of his brother Mark. It is unlikely that there was any love affair between the southern Mark and the former wife of his namesake. He was becoming old and rheumatic and he would spend months at a lodge he had built in Soda Springs in the mountains.

Estelle Latta contends that Mary Sherwood Hopkins was nothing more than a housekeeper to the surviving Mark, but this is improbable for even multimillionaires do not build $3-million homes at a housekeeper's whim. While such a mansion on San Francisco's Nob Hill was being built, Mary was very much in evidence, supervising the construction and playing the role of the mistress who would rule over the castle.

The southern Mark never saw the house completed. In the spring of 1878, he suffered a particularly severe seizure of rheumatism. On March 22, he left San Francisco in a special train, bound for the warm and dry climate of Arizona. His car was put on a siding in Yuma and for a while he appeared to be recovering, but in the evening of March 29, he died in his sleep.

Although many, such as Moses and the three survivors of the Big Four, surely knew that Mary Sherwood Hopkins was the wife of the northern Mark, no one questioned her sudden emergence in the role as the widow of the railroad tycoon. For a while Moses was the executor of the estate; then the courts turned the job over to Mary, who finished the Nob Hill mansion, then started her $2.5 million dolomite castle in Massachusetts.

Estella Latta asserts that the whole affair was part of a vast conspiracy by Stanford, Huntington, and Crocker, who needed Hopkins' money to bolster the sagging finances of the Central Pacific. Despite her nearly lifelong efforts to reclaim the Hopkins estate, few lawyers think she has any chance of success.

"Even if the estate was fraudulently converted," says one San Francisco attorney, "no court is going to take away inherited wealth some five or six generations later."

Perhaps Mary Frances Sherwood did marry the southern

Mark after the conclusion of her affair with Moses. Big Mark may have wished it kept quiet, and he was in a position to see that it was. A peace justice could have been brought to a private railroad car almost anywhere between Yuma and Reno. The certificate could long be buried in some dusty file.

But why did Mary bury her former brother-in-law Ezra and his nephew under false identification? . . . and what ever happened to the northern Mark?

It's all a part of the mysterious West.

13

The Baja View of William Walker

The late Harry Hopkins once said that anything could be sold to the American people so long as it contained the word "freedom." As a nation, we are peculiarly susceptible to semantic inanities. A California politician not so long ago made a thirty-minute speech to a large crowd of cheering supporters in which he developed a thesis that the Freedom from Poverty program was a dire threat to the Free Enterprise System. A Los Angeles politician has been determined that southern Californians shall be given Freedom from Obscenity by fighting a continuing battle against art exhibits and bare-breasted waitresses.

A century ago, "freedom" was not so popular. A large segment of the United States had fought a bitter war for Freedom of the States, and lost, and thus proponents of freedom were generally considered subversives. Successful businessmen saw no stigma attacked to listing their occupations as "capitalist" and those who opposed "manifest destiny" were treated in the same manner as those who object to free enterprise today. It was manifest destiny that led Hopkins and his friends to their financial success, as it was likewise manifest destiny that caused the northern Mark Hopkins to vanish. One of the most avid exponents of manifest destiny was a gentleman by the name of William Walker, who eventually met his death before a Nicaraguan firing squad. Much has been written about this freebooter's activities in Central America, but little has been reported on his activities throughout the mysterious West. It is indeed a mystery as to how such a bumbling buffoon survived long enough to carry out his Nicaraguan invasion. In Central America, the name of William Walker provokes revulsion and hatred. In Baja and northwestern Mexico, the mention results in anything from a smile to a guffaw. As in the case of a television comedian who always gets a laugh by mentioning Brooklyn, yet for no apparent reason, the Mexicans in Baja and Sonora no longer remember why the name of William Walker is funny. But there is a reason.

He was a man of slight build with delicate facial features and a good educational background. He had studied both law and journalism successively in Pennsylvania, Paris, Göttingen, and Heidelberg. After this training, he was employed by a newspaper in New Orleans named the *Crescent*. When the paper folded a short time later, Walker drifted west. For a while, he worked as a newspaperman in San Francisco, then moved on to Marysville where he opened a law practice, taking with him a close friend named Harry Watkins. It was here, with Watkins, that Walker apparently decided that it was his manifest destiny to set up an independent state in Mexico which would be known as the Republic of Sonora and Lower California.

In 1853, posing as newspapermen, Walker and Watkins took a leisurely trip to Mexico, going as far south as Guaymas in Sonora. It was as they anticipated; conditions were deplorable. Yaqui Indian violence posed a constant threat to innocent women and children. The Mexican government was doing nothing to combat this unwarranted aggression by the Yaquis; doing nothing to give these democratic, peace-loving people the protection they deserved. Even the security of the United States was threatened by these warlike savages who, growing bolder every day, soon might sweep across the border and wreak untold horrors upon innocent American women and children. Surely, here was a case of manifest destiny in its finest manifestation. Walker and Watkins headed back toward California, every day becoming more dismayed at the intolerable situation. Even in Tía Juana, just across the border from San Diego, the population lived in constant terror of gangs of marauding bandits. Obviously something had to be done.

The two men returned to San Francisco. Their first act was to float a bond issue to raise money for the treasury of the newly formed and protective Republic of Sonora and Lower California. Walker was the President. Watkins was the Vice-President. A recruiting office was opened. They had little trouble in selling their bonds or raising an army. A large ship named the *Arrow* was purchased to carry Walker and his liberation forces to the new nation. The first objective was the seizure of Baja. Before the expedition could sail, however, the *Arrow* was confiscated by the United States Army under the orders of President Fillmore.

The seizure was considered an outrage in San Francisco, an unwarranted intrusion into the orderly progress of manifest destiny. Many who cared nothing about Walker's project were upset over this arrogant interference on the part of Fillmore. Walker never did recover the *Arrow*, but within two weeks he had raised enough money from sympathizers to acquire a larger ship, the *Caroline*, all of which apparently escaped Fillmore's attention, and Walker sailed unmolested with his army through the Golden Gate on September 30, 1853. His army consisted of forty-six men plus the crew of the ship.

His first invasion was at La Paz in Baja near the tip of the 750-mile-long peninsula. When he dropped anchor in the harbor, small boats put out from shore to ferry the army to land. The Merchants, as usual, were delighted to see a ship in port. The city lay down before the invaders like a trollop. The army strolled over to the governor's palace, arrested that executive, and took him and a box of state documents back to the *Caroline*. The Mexican flag was lowered and replaced by the two-striped banner of Walker's new republic.

Walker then stood on the steps of the governor's piazza and officially proclaimed himself president of the new nation. A few curious residents mingled with the army to hear the proclamation, as beggars and peddlers and pimps hawked their wares to the assemblage. The new state, Walker told his army, would recognize "religious toleration and general protection" and the laws would be based upon the Louisiana Code.

For three days there was a fiesta. The army spent its money in the local cantinas and brothels and then, like many soldiers, retired to the barracks to await their next splurge on the following payday. Then Walker began buying supplies with money drawn on the national treasury of the Republic of Sonora and Lower California; his welcome immediately was worn out in La Paz. Mexican pesos and Yankee dollars were welcome tender but paper Sonoran dollars had no value at all to the citizens of La Paz.

The Mexican Army in La Paz consisted of one man, a

Lieutenant Manual Pineada, who had been left alone by Walker's conquering army because no one knew who he was. When the spending spree was over and the conquerors attempted to buy goods with spurious money, Pineada met with some of the merchants and a decision was reached that the time had come for their guests to depart. There was a problem with the governor who was still a prisoner on the ship, but the consensus was that the governor was only a politician and could easily be replaced.

A counterattack was launched against the invaders. Lt. Pineada did not wish anyone to be hurt seriously, so his attack, led by himself in command of twelve volunteers, consisted of a barrage of sticks and stones against a six-man detail that was returning to the ship with supplies paid for with "Sonoran" money. Walker was incensed over this sudden terrorist activity. Immediately he put ashore some thirty armed men. Lt. Pineada prudently withdrew with his smaller band, but he obviously was upset over the state of affairs and dispatched a message to the Mexican Army detachment stationed at a camp some one hundred kilometers to the north.

Walker interpreted the withdrawal as a signal victory for his troops. When word of the encounter reached San Francisco, Watkins announced the battle in a like vein, commenting that Baja was being released from the tyrannous rule of Mexico and that its people were overjoyed. The untapped mineral and agricultural resources soon would be properly developed with the help of her sister republic above the border, and once the conquest had been consolidated, the new nation would be recognized by the United States government. San Francisco rejoiced. A new ship, the *Anita*, was purchased, and 250 new recruits were enlisted.

Meanwhile, Lt. Pineada had decided that, even with the help of the dozen Mexican Army regulars, the odds still were not in his favor for a direct confrontation with the invaders. He enlisted the help of a prostitute who also was incensed over being paid in Sonoran currency by one of the soldiers. To her next client from Walker's army, she confidentially reported that the Mexican Army detachment to the north was very large, that more than a thousand troops were marching on the city.

President Walker sent word to Vice-President Watkins in San Francisco to speed up the recruiting and told him that, because of military expediency, he was moving the temporary capital of Sonora to Santa Cruz. Then he sailed off with his army and the governor of La Paz. Off the tip of Baja he spotted what appeared to be a warship, so he passed Santa Cruz and put in at Magdalena Bay. The Indians were friendly here and listened to Walker's proclamation, then became unfriendly when the army attempted to buy fruit with paper money.

Walker moved on. His next port of call was Ensenada, less than a hundred kilometers from the United States border. This was a matter of military strategy, he explained in his next message to the Vice-President. He would consolidate the territory close to his line of supply. The good citizens of Ensenada also were delighted to see a fresh ship in port. They clapped and cheered as he led his men in a parade through the community, and he evicted one Pedro Gastelum from the town's finest dwelling to use as his own headquarters, which he named Fort McKibbon. There seemed to be no objection to this because the Gastelums were too rich anyway. Oddly, in Ensenada, the merchants accepted the Sonoran currency, possibly because they were told it was good as a dollar in the United States. Trouble, however, arose on a different front.

Walker dispatched a detail to secure horses, cattle, and food at the La Grulla Ranch, located some distance from the city. The owners of the ranch were justifiably upset over this confiscation and sought help from a notorious bandit in the area named Antonio Melendrez. The bandit gang consisted of some seventy-five men, and they were happy to help their friends at La Grulla. Indeed, a large part of the band used the ranch as a cover for their other activities, posing as farm hands and slipping stolen horses into the ranch herds to hide them. Thus, Melendrez took it as a personal affront when some of his stolen horses were restolen by the Yankee visitors in Ensenada.

As the Walker detachment made its way to Ensenada, it was ambushed by Melendrez' men. Walker's army suffered its first casualty. The rest of the detachment fled and reported this terrorist incident to President Walker at Fort McKibbon. Walker was incensed. He immediately had the army round up the citizens of the town and bring them to Fort McKibbon, where he "talked to the people." He had come only to protect them from the outrages of their own government, he said. His sole objective was the amelioration of their own social and political conditions. By all the arts which conduce to civilization, he continued, he desired to render them free from the curse of the Mexican Republic which was not strong enough to protect them, yet was strong enough to eat up the products of their industry. No bandit would be permitted to disgrace the flag of the new Sonoran Republic, whereas plundering bands of wandering robbers even now were attempting to destroy the saviors.

It was a beautiful speech. A copy of it was sent to Vice-President Watkins, but it arrived many months later. Few persons understood what Walker was saying, and while he was delivering his speech, the Mexican governor from La Paz bribed the skipper of the *Caroline* to take him back home. No sooner had news of this calamity been reported to President Walker, than he was informed that fifty-eight soldiers, pulling a six-pound canon, were headed toward Ensenada from Tía Juana. With the military detachment was the entire band of Antonio Melendrez. The enemies had joined to rid Baja of its savior. There was nothing Walker could do but fight. The army and the bandits were between him and the border, and the *Caroline* was sailing happily toward La Paz.

The encounter was not of long duration. In it Walker suffered thirteen casualties, eight dead and five wounded. The Mexican army detachment lost three men, and one of the bandits was wounded. Melendrez and Colonel Negrete of the Mexican detachment conferred. A fight was not necessary. Walker's men were deployed around the northern edge of the town at the base of two small hills. Between these two hills ran a small stream from which the freebooters were getting their water. A few miles to the east, the stream divided into a Y. It was a comparatively simple matter to post a few snipers on the tops of the hills to keep Walker's men from passing through the canyon back into the city, then dam the tributary of the stream that flowed through his camp.

The seige lasted for eight days, then the desperate President Walker's luck began to change. First, a rare fall thunderstorm swept across the desert. The pressure from the run-off waters collapsed the dam. Under cover of the storm, the freebooters killed three of the hilltop snipers and wounded five others. During the height of the storm, the *Anita* arrived in Ensenada with 250 heavily armed reinforcements for Walker. The solitary cannon of the Mexican Army became bogged down in the Ensenada adobe mud. Negrete and

Melendrez were much too practical to emulate the fabled Spartans. Between them, they had fewer arms and fewer men than the filibustering Walker. With a Latin shrug, they abandoned their cannon and drifted away; Negrete to Tía Juana and a well-deserved vacation in San Diego, and Melendrez back into the mountains with his men. A greatly relieved Walker moved back into his more comfortable Fort McKibbon.

The administration of the new republic lasted three months in Ensenada. Walker admirably played the role required of a head of state. He issued decrees, attended reviews, and through Vice-President Watkins sounded out the United States State Department on the possibility of diplomatic interchange. There were some problems, of course. Three soldiers were accused of undermining the faith of the people in their new currency. Walker had proclaimed that the new Sonoran dollar was worth the same as one Yankee dollar. The three soldiers were buying them at the rate of fifty to one. They were stripped of their stripes and sent back to the United States in disgrace. His greatest problem was Melendrez. Periodically, one of the bandits would pick off a soldier of the republic. Whenever a detachment was sent into the hills to look for Melendrez, however, no trace of him could be found. Walker took a calculated risk. He sent two hundred of his men to comb the area where the bandit was believed to be hidden. While they were gone, Melendrez and his band slipped into Ensenada. They cleaned the army's mess hall of a week's supply of provisions and were gone before the theft was discovered.

Toward the end of the third month, a United States warship, the *Portsmouth*, came into Ensenada Harbor with an answer to Walker's bid for recognition. President Fillmore had no wish to interfere with Walker's manifest destiny, the skipper told President Walker, but would President Walker get the hell out of Ensenada and quit embarrassing the United States government. Walker's alternative, if he did not leave, is not known, but he did decide to accede to Fillmore's wishes. With an announcement that Ensenada would forever be known as the cradle of Sonoran liberty and that this part of the campaign was now well secured, he appointed a grocer as governor general and to him gave the keys to Fort McKibbon. He divided his army into three groups. One he sent to San Vicente and another to El Rosario, to solidify the government in these communities.

The fate of these two detachments is not known, but it is presumed that most of them drifted back to the United States during the ensuing months. The third group, made up of the best one hundred men in the army, came under the personal leadership of President and General Walker and set out for the long and dreary march across the desolate dunes of Camino del Diablo to establish the seat of government for the new republic in Sonora. As soon as he had departed, the governor-general turned back the keys to Fort McKibbon to its original owner, his authority to the old *alcalde*, and went back to his grocery business.

Walker's division consisted of one hundred men, one hundred horses, and one hundred cattle. Most of the animals had been commandeered at the La Grulla ranch. Walker never did discover that this was the hideout for Melendrez. If he had, he might have understood why the indignant bandit and his men trailed his army. By the time the army had crossed the rugged mountains of the peninsula, it had lost two men, four horses, and twenty head of cattle. Not one casualty was suffered by the harassing *bandidos*. The frustrated Walker decided to adopt the practice used by Hernan Cortes when he impressed the Toltecs into his army on the march to Mexico City.

Thus, when the battered Sonoran army emerged on the lowlands and came upon a small Indian village, Walker enlisted thirty Cocopa Indians in the services of his Republic. The Indians were delighted to serve in the cause, Walker reported to his men, which was another indication that all people were tired of the oppression from the Mexican government. The expedition with its new personnel renewed its trek. The following morning, when the army arose, it discovered that all of the Indians had deserted, taking with them thirty head of cattle plus the entire rations for the group. Walker angrily sent a detail back to the Indian village. The detail, carrying two bodies, returned in less than two hours. It had been ambushed by Melendrez.

They reached the Colorado River. A Captain Douglas and a Mr. Smith crossed the stream on the first raft that was built. In his rucksack, Douglas carried a pint of whiskey. Shortly after they reached the other side of the river, Smith stole the whiskey, whereupon Douglas shot him dead. Walker gave Douglas a presidential pardon for his crime. The men drove the cattle into the river in an attempt to force them to swim across. About half of them drowned and were swept into the gulf. That night, as the army camped on the eastern bank of the Colorado, a large segment of the group apparently had second thoughts about its role in Walker's manifest destiny. By morning, fifty-two men had reached a decision. With not so much as a nod to their president, they left the camp and marched north to Fort Yuma in the United States. With more than a thousand miles to go to the seat of the new government, the army of one hundred had dwindled to forty-three and had lost most of its food. President Walker wisely decided that it would be more practical to establish a temporary capital back in Baja at San Vincente.

He lost some more cattle when he recrossed the Colorado River. His band now was smaller than that of Melendrez; forty-seven as compared with the bandit's sixty horsemen. By evening, Walker reached the Rancho Guadalupe of the Osios which he "captured" with no difficulty. Walker decided that his men needed rest and that he should camp here for a few days. The men, however, got little rest. Melendrez hid his men in the rugged terrain surrounding the ranch and kept up a sporadic sniper fire during the night. Shortly after dawn, Walker decided to counterattack and ordered twenty-five men to wipe them out. The snipers prudently withdrew, and the twenty-five-man army set off in purusit.

Melendrez and his bandits then raced into the village from the opposite direction, guns blazing. The eighteen filibusters still in Rancho Guadalupe hid in a small adobe building and watched Melendrez round up the remaining cattle and drive them off toward the mountains. So outnumbered were they, that not one dared fire a shot and so betray his hiding place to the bandit. It was an intelligent decision. The twenty-five man detail sent after the snipers gave up its chase about five miles from the village and turned back. About two miles from the tiny town, they rode into an ambush. Ten more were slain. When the survivors realized they were completely encircled, they threw down their arms and raised their hands in surrender. Melendrez wanted no prisoners, however. He was an honest bandit, not a soldier. He merely took their horses and their pistols and motioned for the survivors to hike back to the village on foot.

For three days, Walker and the thirty-two survivors of his army remained in the Rancho Guadalupe seeing no sign of the dreaded bandit. Then, knowing that he could not remain on the ranch indefinitely, the band marched out onto the desert. They had hiked about ten miles toward San Vicente before they spotted the *bandidos*. This time their behavior seemed different, as if they purposely wanted to be seen: four of them on horseback, motionless with hands resting on the saddle horn. Panic-stricken, the men started to run back in the direction of the ranch, then again halted abruptly. Four other bandits were in the almost identical pose with those in the west. There were none to the north. Slowly and fearfully, the bedraggled survivors began to move in this direction. Within a matter of a few hours it became clear to Walker what Melendrez was doing. Every time Walker attempted to turn his men in the direction of Ensenada or San Vincente, the four horsemen would materialize in the distance. Only when he turned toward the north would they disappear. Melendrez was herding them toward the United States border, almost in the same manner that cattle are driven into a corral.

Some days later, Walker and his army straggled into the bustling border town of Tía Juana. The men had no money; they were hungry and tired. On the outskirts of the city, Walker pulled them all together and to each presented an IOU for back wages and rations allowance drawn on the treasury of the nonexistent republic. He then told them all to cross the border and go back to San Francisco where they would receive further orders. As for himself, Walker said, he would slip through the lines of the enemy and get back to San Vicente.

The men probably were delighted to follow Walker's orders. They split up, avoided the legal point of entry, and slipped back into the United States by wading across the shallow Tía Juana River. Walker, it developed, still had some Yankee dollars in his possession. Whether or not he really planned to attempt to reach San Vincente is unknown. His immediate plans, however, are known. As soon as the last of his men had disappeared, Walker removed the insignia as a general of the Sonoran Republic army from his dusty khaki uniform, walked boldly into the center of the town, and checked into the community's best hotel. His first act here was to order the porter to fetch him the city's best tailor. His second act was to bathe in the hostelry's only tub.

When he returned to his hotel room, Colonel Negrete was sitting on the bed. Also in the room were three Mexican soldiers. The Mexican colonel was in a hurry, so much so that he could not allow Walker time to get dressed. Wearing only a thin summer "union suit," Walker was paraded under guard out of the hotel, into the street. It seemed that the whole town turned out to watch the spectacle. The Mexican men laughed uproariously, and the *señoritas* giggled uncontrollably as the scantily clad Walker was marched to the port of entry at the United States border, where he was arrested by U.S. authorities.

The legend says Colonel Negrete sent Walker's uniform to Melendrez as a souvenir. History does not report the bandit's ultimate fate. Walker and Watkins were tried in San Francisco and found guilty of violating the United States neutrality laws. They were each fined $1,500, but this was allowed to go by default. Oddly, both men were treated as heroes in the City of the Golden Gate. The same treatment was accorded to the men he had left in Tía Juana when they arrived in San Francisco to collect their IOU's. Under these circumstances, they apparently forgot their humiliating experience with a band of Mexican bandits, for when Walker proposed another expedition to liberate the oppressed people of Nicaragua, almost all of the survivors signed on.

Walker's adventures in Nicaragua are much better known than his four-month fiasco in Baja California. He did set himself up successfully as president of that Central American nation, was thrown out of the country, then tried it all over again. The Nicaraguans then became tired of the same old game and ended it by standing Walker up against a wall and filling him with bullets.

The Mexicans of Baja still laugh, however, when they hear the name of William Walker. Although most of them do not know why they have this reaction, it probably goes back to the time when the President of the Republic o Sonora and Lower California was ushered out of the country in his union suit.

14

An Investment in Diamonds

The high mesa country of the United States, sometimes called the roof of the nation, is a large, loosely defined area near the juncture of the states of Utah, Colorado, and Wyoming. It is a desolate section of the West, remote from even small towns, and quite possibly it is because of this remoteness and desolation that it figures so prominently in the mysterious West.

In the northern section of the mesa there is the bogle of little men, so fierce and warlike that some valleys are considered taboo, not only by the Indians but also by shepherds and ranchers. It has long been a lure for treasure seekers. It was in this area that the notorious guide Albert Packer led his party of wealthy eastern prospectors one late fall day. Packer emerged the following spring with a harrowing tale. He was the sole survivor of the party. For months, he reported, they had been trapped by continual blizzards, and eventually, as their supplies ran out, all of the party had succumbed to exposure and starvation, except Packer. What puzzled the natives of Laramie, Wyoming, about Packer's story was that Packer seemed in robust health and his pockets were heavy with money. Some followed Packer's trail back into the mesa country, found his camp, and solved the riddle of the guide's good health and fortune. Packer not only had slain and robbed his companions; he also had butchered and eaten them. To make the story even more bizarre, he escaped any severe punishment for his grisly crime. Jailed safely before he could be lynched by an outraged citizenry, his case was taken up by the then irresponsible Denver *Post*, published by Bonfils and Tammen, to build circulation. The paper so thoroughly confused the facts that Parker eventually was released and is believed to have disappeared in the warrens of the San Francisco Barbary Coast.

The area is best known, however, because of the activities of two opportunistic gentlemen named Philip Arnold and John Slack, both of whom wore the mantle of the rugged western prospector, and one Asbury Harpending, who undoubtedly was one of the most accomplished swindlers of the past century.

Harpending, a native of Kentucky, arrived on the San Francisco scene in 1857. He was a handsome young man with thick, wavy black hair, which he combed to the side. His beard was magnificent, a thick, well-combed bush that he kept trimmed to the level of his coat lapels. His mustache was large and full and trained to grow into his beard. In some pictures, this hirsute growth creates the illusion of a partially masked bandit, but the beard was the style of the times and Harpending was a stylish man. He was always groomed impeccably. His eyes were deeply recessed and radiated sincerity and warmth, a decided asset to any confidence man.

Very little is known about him before his arrival in California. In his memoirs, published in the San Francisco *Bulletin* in 1913, he says that his father was one of the largest landowners in southwestern Kentucky and that in his late teens he joined a company enlisted by William Walker to invade Nicaragua, a unit that was intercepted in New Orleans and disbanded, apparently by the United States Government. In the same series of articles he tells of parlaying a $400.00 stake into a quarter of a million dollars within three years. He described in detail the many "financial coups" he made during his residence in the city, leaving the impression that the Big Four really were the Big Five, with Harpending rounding out the quintet. He was snared once by the authorities, caught leaving the San Francisco harbor aboard the *J. M. Chapman*, with plans to hoist the Jolly Roger and hijack gold from a Pacific Mail steamer. Convicted on charges arising from this conspiracy, he was sentenced to ten years in jail, but served only four months of the sentence.

He claimed close personal friendship with all of the prominent western "capitalists" ranging from Hearst to Le-

land Stanford. It is quite possible that some of these gentlemen recognized a kindred soul in Harpending for there appears to be no record of any of them entering into any kind
of a financial transaction with him, but for one exception,
William C. Ralston, the president of the Bank of California.

Even Ralston must have had some reservations over the
scruples of his charming and debonair friend. There is evidence that he backed away from a deal with Harpending in
Utah involving the allegedly famous Emma Mine. Ralston is
reported to have put up $350,000 for the development of
this underground river of silver but discovered it was a barren hole in the ground before Harpending could get control
of the money.

Harpending decided to unload his mine in an area where
its productivity could not be so quickly determined. He went
to England where he formed the New Mexico Land and
Silver Mining Company, which ostensibly controlled several
mines in the state of New Mexico. Shares in the venture
were put on the market. Before the venture could get underway, it was exposed as a fraud by the London *Times*. The
Emma Mine of Utah was the next project, and this, too,
soon was exposed as a fraud, but apparently not before Harpending had realized a substantial profit, some $35,000 of
which he invested in the purchase of undergrade, or refuse,
diamonds in London. As the name implies, these are stones
of varying sizes that have very little commercial value.

In the fall of 1871, two bearded men dressed in the garb
of the prospector, appeared in the lobby of the Bank of California in San Francisco and insisted upon talking to an
officer of the company. Ushered into the office of George D.
Roberts, they inquired about the cost of renting a box in the
bank's vault. For a while, they acted in a somewhat furtive
manner, enough to pique the curiosity of Roberts, who had
no wish to hide gold taken in a stagecoach robbery or proceeds of a holdup of a competitor.

After some discussion, the two prospectors accepted Roberts' reservations as reasonable, identified themselves as John
Slack and Philip Arnold, and stated that the valuables they
wished to store were diamonds they had discovered while
prospecting for gold.

Slack and Arnold were men of the outdoors and obviously
not familiar with the cunning ways of the financial fraternity. After some additional persuasion by Roberts, they
opened two worn chamois bags and spilled their contents out

onto the desk. The stones were of many sizes and shapes and glittered brilliantly in the shaft of sunlight angling in from the window. There were many, many more where these came from, Arnold said indiscreetly. Some were lying on the surface, others a half inch to two inches beneath the surface.

Roberts readily agreed to rent them a safe deposit box as he watched the two grizzled prospectors sweep their precious stones back into the sacks. Of course, he explained, he would need an address to note on the receipt. Arnold and Slack were barely out of the bank before Roberts was relating his experience to William C. Ralston. The two bankers were fascinated with the story and that evening trailed the two prospectors to their modest rooms on the Embarcadero.

Neither Arnold nor Slack was very communicative. They would give no clue as to the location of their find except to say that it was about a thousand miles away. Both appeared somewhat simple-minded, bewildered by their good fortune. They had no plans other than to sell their diamonds as they needed funds, then return to their field and harvest some more. Both agreed that they liked and trusted Mr. Ralston and Mr. Roberts and also readily agreed to meet with them again.

In the ensuing week or ten days, Ralston met with the two men daily. If they continued with their present plans, Ralston explained, they were taking a great risk of losing everything. They would be followed back to their discovery, because news of such a fabulous find could not forever be kept secret. There also was the possibility that someone else might stumble upon the find. If the crop of diamonds was harvested in the proper manner, however, Philip Arnold and John Slack would have the limitless wealth of Mark Hopkins or Collis Huntington.

Eventually the two prospectors began to melt under the charm of the banker. If Ralston would take care of the legalities of staking a claim and underwrite the costs of mining the diamonds, then Arnold and Slack would be willing to sell a half-interest in their discovery. Another snag. Ralston was willing to buy such a half-interest but first he must know the location of the mines. The two prospectors adamantly refused. Again there was a long period of persuasiveness on the part of Ralston before an agreement was reached. Arnold and Slack would take two men, selected by Ralston, to the diamond fields, but both must agree to be blindfolded on the way in and on the way out.

Just who Ralston chose for this assignment is unknown. One report identifies one of the men as David D. Colton, an executive of the Central Pacific Railroad. The other generally is believed to be Roberts. It is unknown also whether or not the trip was made immediately before the onslaught of the heavy winter snows or in the spring, after the snows had melted and were racing toward the Gulf of California in the Colorado River. It is known that the party did return to San Francisco with more diamonds, and coincident with their return was the arrival of Asbury Harpending in the city. In his memoirs, Harpending says that he was asked to return by Ralston to get in on the bonanza.

Apparently there still was some doubt as to the total value of the find. Arnold and Slack could understand this and both agreed to return to the diamond fields once again, this time returning "with a million dollars' worth of diamonds."

This trip was made in record-breaking time. When they returned they were accompanied by Harpending who "to share in the heavy burden of responsibility" had met them on the return trip near Reno. There had been a slight mishap, Arnold reported apologetically. They had placed the diamonds in two sacks, and the larger had been lost while fording a stream. Both prospectors also were exhausted, so much so that they had left the train at Oakland to check into a hotel, entrusting the remaining diamonds to Harpending. However, even the remaining sack contained $250,000 worth of the precious stones, Harpending assured Ralston and some of the banker's friends when he displayed the diamonds later that evening.

The next stage is the most difficult to understand. An expert appraisal of the value of the diamonds was needed, and the leading expert in the nation was Tiffany of New York. The delegation chosen to carry the gems to New York consisted of Arnold, Slack, and Harpending. Tiffany appraised the samples shown to him by the trio as worth $150,000. If the gems in San Francisco were of equal value to the random samples shown Tiffany, they were worth approximately $1.5 million. Nevertheless, there still was some hesitancy among the bankers. All that was needed now to consummate the deal, they said, was the report of an expert consulting engineer who would visit the fields. The expert chosen for this task was one Henry Janin, a prominent consulting engineer of conservative reputation.

At this point, Arnold and Slack became somewhat balky,

but their reticence was overcome finally when they were paid $100,000 as an advance for their sale of half-interest. There was another proposal to which the prospectors would not agree. Ralston wanted Roberts and some other representatives of the bank to meet Janin, Harpending, Arnold, and Slack in Omaha and accompany them to the diamond fields. Harpending agreed with the prospectors that would indeed be a matter of bad faith and thus Roberts was turned back.

The quartet left the train at Rawlins, Wyoming, in the high mesa country of the United States, proceeded southwest through Baggs, Wyoming, then on to an area in the extreme northwestern part of Colorado now known as Brown's Park. Many other areas of the West have claimed identification with the site of Arnold and Slack's diamond mines, such as Shakespeare, New Mexico, but there is no doubt as to its location in Colorado. Many of these other claims undoubtedly stem from the rush of prospectors into New Mexico and Arizona, after the find was announced, in the belief they knew the general area of the fields.

Closely supervised by Janin, the quartet began its search. Within a few minutes the first diamond had been unearthed, and within a few hours a chamois sack had been filled. By the end of the first day, Janin was convinced, so much so, that he prevailed upon Arnold and Harpending to leave Slack behind to guard the treasure until the proper claims could be filed and appropriate security measures taken.

All doubt was dispelled in San Francisco. As soon as Janin's report was accepted, Ralston began to put together his corporation. Twenty-five men of the city's business community were called together, given the evidence and each bought $80,000 worth of stock for an initial capitalization of $2 million. The board of directors included William C. Ralston, who also was named treasurer. David C. Colton gave up his position with the Big Four's Central Pacific Railroad to become general manager. Harpending, who claimed that he was called back from England to take part in the venture, and who worked so actively in its promotion, was not placed on the board nor given a position in the new organization which was named the San Francisco and New York Mining and Commercial Company. Arnold, however, was given another $400,000 advance for his interest. Janin was named general superintendent of the project. The publicity began to pour out from the company and was picked up by newspapers all over the world. The stock was prepared for listing on the New York Exchange.

A plush suite of offices for the company was set up in San Francisco and on the wall of the lobby was a huge map in bas-relief showing the more than three thousand acres claimed by the San Francisco and New York Mining and Commercial Company. Concessions on a small piece of the field were offered, and believed sold, although there are no known records of such concession purchases now in existence. The company was organized on July 30, and it was the plan of the Board of Directors to let a three-month period elapse before a public offering of the stock was made. The delay was designed to raise speculator interest to a fever pitch by the time they were allowed to buy into the fabulous diamond mine. So extensive was the publicity that it penetrated one of the more rural areas of Colorado and caught the attention of one Clarence King who was conducting a survey for the United States government.

The skeptical geologist found the diamond field with little difficulty, although his success in so doing has never been made clear. There was nothing in the geological history of the area that could account for the presence of the precious gems in this most remote mesa. He went there expecting to find nothing and he was most puzzled when he "washed up" some of the stones. When he had acquired a fair sampling, he spread them out on his blanket and examined them closely under a powerful magnifying glass. Presently he broke out into laughter. One of the larger specimens had been cut by a lapidary. Before the stone had been "mined" it had been in the hands of a jeweler. Once again King went through the fields. This time he found the evidence he sought. Three holes had resisted the smoothing hand of time, showing definite evidence of being manmade. Someone had taken a crowbar, driven it into the ground, dropped a diamond in it, then tamped it shut, probably with a boot heel. The salting had been done at least a year earlier, possibly two, and the snows, the rains, and the wind had restored most of the field to its original state.

King rode into Rawlins, Wyoming, where he dispatched a telegram to the San Francisco and New York Mining and Commercial Company, informing them that their mine had been salted with cheap refuse diamonds and that at least one of them had been cut by the lapidary. The board of directors was concerned, to put it mildly, and became even more upset when they discovered that the Associated Press considered King's assertions most newsworthy.

King was contacted immediately, and he readily agreed to take a group back into the field and prove his assertions. The company delegated four of its members, including Henry Janin, but not Asbury Harpending, to make the trip with King.

The inspection party returned to San Francisco on November 25. Two days later, the San Francisco and New York Mining and Commercial Company was dissolved. There was considerable wake in the folding of the company, and many questions have been left unanswered even to this day. No one can understand how Tiffany's, the epitome of integrity, could appraise a sack of refuse diamonds as being worth $150,000. John Slack vanished as completely as did the Mark Hopkins of New York. He was last seen guarding the salted diamond field on the high mesa of Colorado. There is no answer to how a man of such high integrity as Henry Janin could have been so easily duped.

That Ralston suspected Harpending as a part of the plot is evinced by the banker's sending the refuse diamonds to England in the hopes that they could be traced there. He was partially successful. A diamond merchant there identified the diamonds as part of a lot he had sold to an American about two years previously. The transaction had been in cash, however, and the merchant could not identify Harpending as his customer.

Harpending contended that he was an innocent victim of the swindle; detectives backtracked Arnold's movement and found that he had made two trips to London about two years earlier. In his memoirs, however, Harpending clearly shows his bitterness toward Clarence King, and it can be assumed that this must stem from the role King played in establishing the diamond mine as a hoax.

Although millions were lost by the premature exposure, the swindlers did not wind up in the red. With an investment of $35,000 they collected more than $600,000. Arnold returned to his native Kentucky and was followed there by Harpending, also a native of the same state. A suit was filed against Arnold in an attempt to recover the $600,000, but it was unsuccessful. Ironically, Arnold opened a bank with his share of the loot, but he did not live long to enjoy his prosperity. He was shot during an argument with a competitive banker, and while bedridden from his wounds, he caught pneumonia and died.

Harpending moved back to California, lived in Oakland for a while where he wrote his memoirs for a series in the San Francisco *Bulletin.* Later he moved to New York, where he died in 1923. Ralston's Bank of California collapsed a few years after the diamond hoax, and two days after its failure he died of an apparent heart attack while swimming at North Beach.

The high mesa country of the diamond field never has dropped into limbo. As testimony to the hoax, there is Diamond Mountain. For years, it was a perfect hideout for the badman of the West, and one bad woman known as Queen Ann Bassett, none of whose exploits are worthy of mention in this volume. After World War II, the area came up with a real treasure, uranium, and some claims were staked on the exact site of the salted diamond mine.

As recently as October 1966, the site of the salted diamond mine figured luridly, but briefly, in the news and came up with a secret that surely would have caused the late Asbury Harpending to gnash his teeth in frustration. Bert Hanna of the Denver *Post* reported that Roy Leatherman of Waldon, Colorado, and a group of associates had filed about 1,200 claims in the area. Leatherman was quoted as saying that positive samples taken from the area showed recoverable platinum ore worth at least $40 a ton, and that it averaged 929 tons per square mile. With platinum presently selling for $110 per ounce, it made the site of the old diamond field worth $37 billion per square mile.

Once again, an agent of the U.S. Geological Survey visited the area. An analysis of the land did indeed show the presence of platinum and gold and one tiny refuse diamond. The more than two thousand persons who had rushed to stake claims in the area, however, were overly optimistic on the yield. The platinum and gold were in such small proportions that they could not possibly be mined at a profit.

It is ironic, nevertheless, that Asbury Harpending salted his diamond mine in a field of platinum and gold . . . and never knew it.

15

The Baron of Arizona

The long, luxury Southern Pacific train from Los Angeles to the East was longer than usual on the Saturday night of September 2, 1882, although now there is no known reason as to why so many persons were traveling on this date. It was an exceptionally warm night, but this was not unusual; in Arizona, the warmest days of the year often come in September. The windows of the train were wide open as most of the travelers far preferred the hot moving air of the desert over a still, sweaty interior, even though the former choice brought with it an occasional billow of black smoke from the speeding locomotive at the head of the train. With four exceptions, history has kept no record of those who found it necessary to travel across the desert this night.

The exceptions are a Mr. and Mrs. House who some years earlier had traded a New England farm for a Tucson ranch, had done well financially and apparently considered sexual intercourse the most frightful crime; a very pretty French maid just hired in Los Angeles by House, named Marie Delacroix, and a James Addison Reavis, a well-dressed debonair man of thirty-nine years who was known as the Baron of Arizona.

The brief and passionate romance between Marie Delacroix and the Baron of Arizona apparently began when the baron gallantly removed a cinder from the eye of the French maid. Apparently, Mrs. House became suspicious of her maid and the baron, and for the sake of God and morality she followed them from one end of the train to the other during the long hot afternoon and early evening. Her suspicions continued after the porters had made up the berths, becoming so strong that she eventually crept from her bed to check on Marie. When Mrs. House pulled apart the curtains to Marie's berth, she found her worst suspicions confirmed, but to witness them actually committing the crime was too much for the moralistic Mrs. House. She screamed loudly, calling her husband, until he jumped into the corridor; then she promptly swooned. Other defenders of the fair sex piled into the corridor, and the resulting melee lasted for the better part of an hour before the conductors were able to get everyone, including the baron, back in his own bed.

The next morning, when these four alighted from the Southern Pacific's Overland at Tucson, Marie Delacroix was left at the station to catch the next train to Los Angeles. James Addison Reavis was arrested upon the insistence of Mrs. House, but released a short time later after payment of a small fine.

It was on such a note that James Addison Reavis arrived in Arizona to lay claim to his land grant which consisted of approximately 90 per cent of the Arizona Territory and a large hunk of the New Mexico Territory. The claim extended 235 miles east and west and 75 miles north and south, a total of 7,500 square miles, or 12 million acres. It included the cities of Phoenix, Maricopa, Casa Grande, Mesa, Florence, Safford, Globe, and Clifton; a few miles of the Southern Pacific Railroad, numerous silver and copper mines, and hundreds of ranches. The claim was a fraud, but before it was so indicated, scores of ranchers and businessmen, including Charles Crocker of California's Big Four, had paid large sums to Reavis for quit claim deeds.

What is even more amazing, and a part of the mysterious West, is that a few years after Reavis was practically run out of the territory, he returned. The second time he carried papers that proved his earlier claim was fraudulent but at the same time provided the basis for another attempt to pick up title to the same 7,500 square miles. And again, miners and ranchers and businessmen came up with money for Reavis to quit his claim on their property.

Reavis most definitely had a variety of talents and a most engaging personality, which are the basic requirements of the successful confidence man. He was born in Missouri, the son of a merchant-farmer, and served in the Civil War in the armies of both the North and the South. It was while in the military that he discovered one of his greatest talents—the gentle art of forgery.

Donald M. Powell, of the University of Arizona, tells of an incident involving Reavis along these lines in his book, *The Peralta Grant,* published by the University of Oklahoma Press. While serving in the Confederate army, Reavis discovered that he could imitate his commanding officer's signature almost to perfection. He discovered it was more practical to forge a pass than to fight. When the fortunes of the Confederate army appeared bleak, he forged himself some furlough papers and took off for the winners in the North.

There are varying reports concerning his activities immediately following the war. Some say he went to Brazil and Central America. The latter is possible because he showed a speaking fluency in Spanish. For a while, he lived in St. Louis, Missouri, dealing in real estate profitably. His specialty was in buying properties with imperfect titles, applying his talents to the papers, then selling them with perfect titles which substantially increased their value. On one such transaction he became careless, and as a result, he departed hurriedly for California where he found employment as a high-school teacher in the small community of Downey near Los Angeles. It was here that apparently he was given the idea to press a claim to most of the Territory of Arizona.

Near Downey was a small ranch owned by a man named Horace Bell who was a close friend of another rancher in the area named William Reynolds. At one time Reynolds had lived in Arizona near Casa Grande, and he had written a novel whose central character was a conquistador known as Miguel Peralta whose holdings were so vast that he was known as the Baron of Arizona. Reynolds had spent a considerable effort developing a plausible background for his fictional nobleman, Peralta, and more than three years writing his novel. Written in longhand, there was only one copy. Before sending it to the prospective publisher, Reynolds wanted some expert criticism of the work and he mentioned his problem to Bell. The rancher knew just the man, the gregarious and intellectual high-school teacher in Downey, James Addison Reavis. The manuscript was delivered to Reavis. Some weeks later, Reynolds went to Downey. Reavis was distraught. Before he had read the manuscript, indeed the very day after he had received it, thieves had broken into his home and made off with the work as well as other valuable papers. Reynolds' work of three years was lost, but

Miguel Peralta, the man he invented along with his fictional ancestors, was destined to achieve a fame far greater than their creator had imagined.

The treaty that ended the war between Mexico and the United States contained a clause in which the United States agreed to recognize the validity of Mexican and Spanish land grants within the ceded territory. The United States government had set up special land offices throughout the Southwest to check the validity of such grants. The recognition of these by the government has provided the base of many a fortune, particularly in southern California.

When speculating in real estate in St. Louis, Reavis had conducted several transactions with a Dr. Juan Gid, a renegade attorney from Mexico, who was a "specialist" in Spanish land grants in that area. With Reynolds' novel presumably tucked in his valise, Reavis gave up his teaching career in Downey and headed back to Missouri for a meeting with Gid. Apparently Gid thought the novel was excellent, but before any profit could be realized on the Peralta land grant of twelve million acres, some method must be devised to convey the title to Reavis. This problem was overcome with the help of an aging prospector named George M. Willing, Jr.

Willing turned out to be ideal in his role. He had prospected in Arizona, was known around Prescott, and was willing to go along with the scheme. He memorized his story and it followed these lines:

—Many years earlier, while prospecting in Arizona, he had heard of the huge Peralta land grant. One day he found the Peraltas living in a remote mining camp near Prescott. The Peraltas, a son named Miguel, and an aging father, were nearly destitute and were happy to sell their claim to Willing for the money he carried with him. The transaction was consummated and its details written on a dirty piece of wrapping paper for $20,000 worth of gold.—

Willing was given the "bill of sale," an assortment of Spanish documents provided by Gid, and sent off to Prescott where he recorded the deed in the Yavapai County Courthouse conveying a land grant from Miguel Peralta to himself. Willing never got back to St. Louis to transfer the deed to Reavis. The morning after he filed the deed he was found dead in a Prescott rooming house.

Reavis waited several months for the return of the old prospector, during which time he married. At the expiration of six months, Reavis apparently gave up his vigil, kissed his wife goodbye, and left for San Francisco. (She was more patient than her husband. She waited six years before she divorced him.)

In San Francisco, Reavis became a reporter for the *Examiner,* later the *Call,* and there appears to be no doubts over his competency as a journalist. He became a correspondent for several New York papers; later, he founded his own weekly publication in Sacramento. His tenure as a journalist is vague, but it is known that sometime in either 1879 or 1880, he came to Phoenix ostensibly to write a series of feature stories for his paper on the Arizona Territory. During this visit, he caught a stage to Prescott apparently to check up on the missing Willing.

After a rough, twenty-four hour trip, he arrived in the frontier town, again posing as a working newspaperman. He discovered that the deed had been filed, and that Willing had died the following day. Continuing his investigation, he soon found the judge who had presided over the coroner's jury ruling on Willing's death. To him he presented a forged letter from Willing's widow authorizing him to take possession of the dead man's effects. He was lucky. Willing's possessions still had been kept in a gunny sack, and in the inside pocket of a frayed overcoat Reavis found the forged deed which laid claim to the Peralta land grant.

There still was the problem of having the dead man's deed transferred to him. The most simple manner to accomplish this would be to buy it from Willing's widow, but apparently Reavis did not think such an easy solution was the best. It was too simple perhaps for his talents, or possibly he thought it would look better to confuse the chain of possession. Again, he might have thought the widow would be too hard to handle. He solved the problem by going first to Kentucky where, for a small fee, he did secure a power of attorney from Mary Willing to act on her behalf in all matters pertaining to her husband's estate. At the same time he convinced her that she should assign the deed to an old friend of the dead prospector's, a Florin Massol who was a small merchant in Sacramento. The gregarious confidence man then returned to Sacramento where, with no difficulty, he purchased the spurious deed from Massol for $3,000.

Reavis most certainly was a patient man. For such a fraud

to be successful would need many more papers and documents than the comparatively few in his possession. The next step, and the most important, was to establish the existence of the fictitious Peralta family and to divorce it from the aristocratic Peraltas of Sonora, Mexico, who, a few years earlier, had operated a gold mine north of Sutter's Creek. The technique he adopted utilized his greatest talent. Still using the unpublished novel as his guide, Reavis went first to Washington where an exhibition of books and documents from an old Tucson mission were on display. Still playing the role of a newspaperman, he was granted permission to examine the mission books closely. Into this collection he planted several forged papers relating to the lineage of the Peraltas and the vast properties that they owned in New Spain. The next step was to call in a photographer to copy the "discovered" documents, and to obtain certification that such documents were in the files.

He went to Mexico City and Guadalajara where the archivists welcomed him as a charming North American journalist and, delighted that he was writing a series for several United States papers on Mexican history, dug out countless bundles of dusty old documents for him to study. Some of the documents were altered, others removed, and new forgeries were inserted. The fictional hero of William Reynolds was gaining substance.

No longer was he merely the Don Miguel Peralta, the Baron of Arizona. His full name, as prepared by Reavis, was Don Miguel Nemecio Silva de Peralta de la Cordoba. His father was Don José Gaston Silva y Carrillo de Peralta de las Falces de Mendoza and his mother was the Doña Francisca María de García de la Cordoba y Muñez de Pérez y Velázquez. Born in Spain, he was sent, when in his middle thirties, to Guadalajara, as a personal inspector for King Philip V of Spain and given a few titles including those of the Order of the Montesa, Knight of the Golden Fleece, and Baron of Arizonaca. The second title would have been particularly appropriate had Reavis been successful in his prosecution of the claim.

After the character of Don Miguel was established, Reavis "found" the huge land grant in the files of the Guadalajara archives. Don Miguel officially staked out his claim in 1758. This was documented also. In the files of the San Xavier Mission there was a report of a Father Francisco Pauer who had accompanied Don Miguel's weeks-long surveying party.

A wife of the fictitious Don Miguel was invented and she in turn had a fictitious son and the strain was carried on to the two Peraltas, father and son, who had been found, impoverished, by Willing in the remote mining camp near Prescott, Arizona. These, the last of the Peraltas, had returned to the Mexican State of Jalisco with their $20,000 where both perished while on a hunting trip after their horses shied on a narrow mountain path. By coincidence, the accident occurred when Reavis was conducting his research in the Guadalajara archives and it was only by chance that he noticed the small report of the incident in the newspapers.

With this mass of evidence, including a few oil paintings of the original Peraltas and his "dirty deed" obtained by Willing, Reavis set forth for Tucson on the Southern Pacific Overland in September 1882, dallied happily with the French maid of Mrs. House, and was arrested as he came to claim his holdings.

As soon as he was released from jail, Reavis filed his claim with the United States Surveyor General in Tucson, a necessary action in the processing of Mexican or Spanish land grants. The filing of the deed by Willing in Prescott had been unnoticed by the press. Such was not the case in the filing by Reavis with the U.S. Surveyor General. The citizens of the Territory of Arizona suddenly realized that their status could easily have changed from that of owner to squatter and that it was equally possible that they enjoyed no rights in the latter category.

The newspapers from one end of the territory to the other raised a bitter outcry. "What are you going to do about it?" queried the Arizona *Gazette*. ". . . Your course must be peace or war . . . this danger is imminent and prompt action is demanded."

Reavis was not upset. He called a press conference to announce that he would deal reasonably with the settlers on his lands and that in no case would he charge more than three dollars per acre for the land on which they were living. Within the matter of a few weeks, Reavis certainly had recovered his expenses. He sold quit claim deeds to mining companies, railroads, and ranchers from one end of the territory to the other. One of the sales was to the publisher of the Arizona *Gazette*, a transaction which was discovered by a rival newspaper, the *Herald*, which promptly labeled the *Gazette* "a Reavis organ." The embarrassed publisher then tore up his quit claim deed. For almost two years, Reavis wandered throughout the territory, picking up thousands upon thousands of dollars for his deeds. Even Charles Crocker, one of California's Big Four, gave Reavis a check for $5,000 for a right of way across the baronial estate.

The sales then abruptly came to a halt because of a development that the debonair confidence man understandably had failed to anticipate. Unknown to Reavis was the fact that Willing had a father in Philadelphia who still was alive. This fact was known to Gid, back in St. Louis, who apparently was unhappy over the division of the profits. Gid arranged for a St. Louis lawyer named Britton Hill to get together with George Willing, Sr. A will was found in Philadelphia which indicated that the dead prospector had left his estate to his wife only for the remainder of her life and upon her death the remainder of the estate was to revert to the Willings of Pennsylvania. Hill filed suit to have the courts nullify Reavis' claim and arranged to have offices opened in Phoenix which could sell legitimate quit claim deeds to the huge Peralta land grant, on the grounds that only the senior Willing could offer such a deed.

Reavis was trapped in an impossible situation. The will was legitimate. The widow had no authority to sign the transfer deed to the fraudulent claim. She did not know that it was fraudulent, nor did her father-in-law and his lawyers. Indeed, it surely must have been a frustrating few weeks for Reavis as he faced the possibility that the proceeds from the swindle over which he had labored for years might go to another. The only way he could see to stop it was to label it as a swindle, but the least he could hope from this was a jail term on a fraud conviction. He was given a respite, however, from an unexpected quarter.

The help came from the citizens themselves. The newspapers pointed out succinctly that there possibly could be no end to the sale of quite claim deeds. If Reavis' claim could be contested by Willing, then so in turn could Willing's claim by still another party. Residents in the Territories of Arizona and New Mexico could be bled by a series of claimants for generations. The newspapers urged mass rallies to demand that the government of the United States make a ruling immediately. The citizens responded quickly, and their mood was ugly and hostile. One such rally was held in Phoenix, and leaders of the milling crowd discovered that Reavis was presently staying at one of the city's hotels. As the crowd began to gather outside of the hotel, Reavis quietly packed his belongings, slipped out the rear entrance, and caught the next train heading west.

The rallies had another salutary effect for Arizonians. Word of the rising tempers in the territory had reached Washington, and the Congress applied pressure to Land Office Commissioner W. A. Sparks. He, in turn, wrote to the surveyor general in Tucson reprimanding him for his futile work of some two years in studying the validity of the claim and ordered him to disregard the entire matter. Arizonians and New Mexicans were jubilant. It was typical of the frontier attitude that no one went after Reavis for revenge. The issue was dead, they thought, but they had underestimated the tenacity of Reavis.

The Baron of Arizona still wanted his 7,500-square-mile estate, and a new approach was necessitated. The Willing approach obviously was as dead as the man for whom it was named. Yet the large files of papers, certified copies, and photographs, the forged insertions into the archives at Washington and Guadalajara, which "proved" the existence of a Don Miguel Peralta, had not been challenged seriously, and thus could be used in the next go-around.

Reavis came up with his answer very shortly after his flight from Phoenix. To him, it surely seemed foolproof. He would marry a direct descendant of the Peraltas who also would be the only Peralta still living. At the same time, the two Peraltas who had been found destitute in the small mining camp near Prescott would be "proved" as confidence men who had taken a gullible prospector of his life savings.

About three weeks after leaving Arizona, Reavis boarded a Central Pacific train at Oakland, headed for Sacramento. On the same train was a beautiful Mexican lass who bore a striking resemblance to a portrait of one of the Peralta women, a portrait acquired by Reavis during his years of research into the origins of the Peralta family.

Reavis, his story continued, was so entranced by the likeness that he approached the young woman, and by the time the train had reached Sacramento he learned that the girl was an orphan; that her father had died while on a visit to Cadiz when she was a child and that she had been cared for by a Captain Snowball who ran a small farm outside of Sacramento. Reavis immediately launched an investigation into her background, not only because of his interest in

Peralta, but because of his increasing love for the beautiful and aristocratic young woman.

Almost immediately, he found evidence that the Willing deed was worthless. The two Peraltas that Willing had found in the mining camp had been imposters. The real heir to the Peralta grant, one Don Jesús Miguel Peralta, had married a Doña Juana Laura Ibarra in Guadalajara in 1822 and had given birth to a daughter, Sophia Laura Micaela de Peralta de la Cordoba y Ibarra. When Sophia was in her late twenties, she married a José Ramón Carmen Maso, son of a prominent Spanish family from Cadiz. The marriage, alas, was beset by tragedy and short-lived. José was summoned home to Cadiz shortly after the honeymoon. Don Jesús, shortly after José's departure, decided to inspect some properties he owned in northern California and took the pregnant Sophia along on the trip. In San Bernardino, before they reached their destination, Sophia gave birth to twins, a boy and a girl, prematurely. The boy and his mother perished. The daughter survived.

The sorrowing Don Jesús went on to San Francisco with his granddaughter and here he arranged for her to be raised with the family of a dear friend named John Treadway in Sherwood Valley. No sooner had this arrangement been finalized, than Don Jesús was summoned urgently to Cadiz by José on business. Before he departed, he took the precaution of executing a will which left the Peralta land grant to his infant granddaughter. Again tragedy struck. When he arrived in Cadiz, he learned that the girl's father had died. A few weeks later, Don Jesús was stricken with a fatal malady. Then Treadway passed on and the Baroness of Arizona, still an infant and thus unaware of her great inheritance, wound up in the custody of Captain John Snowball, also of Sherwood Valley. Even Captain Snowball was unaware of his ward's noble lineage. He had thought her to be the daughter of Treadway and an attractive Indian lass with whom Treadway had lived for a while. He was "most amazed" when Reavis presented him with evidence found in mission records in San Bernardino, that Sophia Treadway was in reality Doña Sophia Loreta Micaela Maso y Peralta de la Cordoba, that she had been so baptized and that she was the heiress to a vast fortune.

The will made by Don Jesús in San Francisco mysteriously was missing, but Reavis was positive that the meticulous Spaniard would have filed a copy of the will in Spain prior to his death. He was equally sure that there would be other documents in Madrid to support Doña Sophia's claim to Arizona, and so convinced a New York millionaire, John W. Mackay, who agreed to underwrite research expenses in Spain for Reavis and his "ward" plus a $500 subsistence allowance monthly. Shortly after his arrival in Europe, Reavis married the Doña Sophia. His beloved acquired a seventh name and somehow in the transaction, Reavis acquired a fourth. From this time on, he referred to himself as James Addison Peralta-Reavis.

In Spain, however, Reavis found it more difficult to build the file on the Peralta land grant. Quite possibly because of his success in planting phony documents in the files of the United States and Mexico, he became careless through over-confidence. For several months, he enjoyed his honeymoon at Mackay's expense before he once again turned his attention to the project to which he had devoted so many years. He stumbled on his first attempt.

With Doña Sophia he appeared at the Archives of the Indias at Seville and successfully talked the officials into letting him examine the files. A few days later, he requested a copy of a document he had noticed. A clerk, complying with the request, reported that he had never seen such a document before and that he believed it to be a plant.

Reavis was given the copy he sought, but when he next appeared in the library his every movement was under surveillance. This time he was caught as he slipped another forged document into the files and thrown out of the building. A criminal complaint was filed against him, but before he could be arrested, Reavis had fled and was sailing back to the United States with his baroness. A few months later, he was caught doing the same thing in Guadalajara, but again he escaped before he could be arrested.

It is odd that Reavis saw no great obstacle to his plans over the incidents. On September 2, 1887, he came into Tucson quietly, filed a plethora of documents with the United States Surveyor General supporting his claim to the Peralta land grant and at the same time, asking the government to conduct a survey of the grant. This time, however, Reavis wasted no time traveling throughout the two territories to sell quit claim deeds to apprehensive corporations and ranchers. Instead he launched the Casa Grande Improvement Company with an initial capitalization of $50 million. The company would undertake a vast irrigation program throughout the Peralta land grant that would result in the creation of the largest cattle and crop raising ranch in the world. One newspaper referred to the proposed ranch as the "garden of the world." President of the new corporation was none other than the internationally famous attorney, Robert Ingersoll. Incorporators included the cream of the American capitalistic society from New York to San Francisco: men such as Dwight Townsend, David Ferguson, and Henry Porter. His attorney was Senator Roscoe Conkling, and another supporter of the corporation and Reavis' claim was Congressman James Broadhead. How Reavis suddenly acquired this respectability has never been determined. Apparently his income was great during the next three years. With the Doña Sophia, he traveled steadily between San Francisco, New York, and Washington, wearing the most expensive clothes and living in the most luxurious hotel suites. The caliber of the promoters of the Casa Grande Company was so great that it gave credence to the mass of documents Reavis had acquired. A majority of Arizonians and New Mexicans began to believe that the claim was indeed valid. Many sought out Reavis' attorneys to beg for a quit claim deed. The Silver King Mining Company paid $25,000 for such a document, and the Southern Pacific Railroad wrote out another check. Homes within the grant could not be sold because the title was clouded. Only one hurdle remained to be cleared before Peralta-Reavis assumed control of his 475-square-mile estate. This was recognition of the claim by the United States Land Commissioner's Office. Not only was no action being taken on the claim, but the surveyor general had not even taken the initial steps to survey the claim. Reavis offered to post $10,000 to help defray the costs of the survey, but not only did the surveyor fail to accept such a generous offer—he did not even acknowledge the letter in which the offer was made. To the Baron of Arizona, this was a gross insult which could not be overlooked. The best remedial action was to sue the government. In 1890, the irate Reavis sued the United States for $6 million, charging that the government had sold thousands of acres of land that rightfully belonged to him, had illegally expropriated more than a million acres for its own use, and had even taken water from the Gila River that rightfully belonged to Reavis.

It took almost five years, however, before the case finally came to court. With the action pending, the Casa Grande

Improvement Company remained in limbo, but Reavis still appeared to be abundantly well financed. Reavis spent the time tidying up the small details in his case. He found new witnesses in San Francisco who could tie the Doña Sophia in with Don Jesús and, somewhere in Mexico, an "agent" at last located the long missing will of Don Jesús which gave the Peralta grant to his wife. When the trial opened on June 3, 1895, in Santa Fe, New Mexico, it was a most confident Reavis who appeared with more than three cases of documents to support his claim. When the court opened for business, however, Reavis failed to appear. The five justices summoned to preside over the court did not seem perturbed over Reavis' absence. They merely ordered the government to go ahead with its case.

It is unlikely that Reavis was not informed of the developments in the prosecution's case. In the half-decade it had taken to prepare its case, the government had been most thorough. Investigators had been sent to both Madrid and Mexico. They testified as to the arrest warrants outstanding against Reavis in both countries for falsifying records. His witnesses appeared as government witnesses to tell of Reavis' chicanery, and at least one indicated he was motivated because of Reavis' failure to pay him as had been agreed. A padre from the San Bernardino mission appeared to swear that the baptismal certificate of Doña Sophia's was a forgery; that it appeared in only one of the two sets of books maintained by the mission.

Perhaps even more humiliating for Reavis was the fact that he did not excel in his most cherished talent of forgery. Some of the documents had been forged with a steel pen, a device unknown when the documents allegedly were drawn. One of the papers, reportedly written by the king of Spain, contained three grammatical errors in six lines, plus an equal number of spelling errors. The most telling evidence against Reavis, however, was the testimony from Mexican and Spanish officials, by deposition, that no evidence could be found anywhere of the existence of a Don Miguel Peralta other than in documents that were well proven as forgeries. It took the government five days to destroy the elaborate façade that it had taken Reavis fifteen years to build.

When Reavis finally appeared in court, he came as his own attorney, and he was a badly shaken man. His answers were evasive, and on several occasions he was excused from the court on his own request. One such request came after it was developed in his examination that John Treadway, the man who Reavis claimed had brought up his wife, had died about six months before the Doña Sophia was born.

Before the trial was over, Reavis had lost all of his support. The court understandably declared the Reavis claim a fraud, and before he could leave his hotel he was arrested on a charge of attempting to defraud the government. He was penniless. He could not raise the $500 bail.

Upon his conviction of this charge, he was sentenced to the Federal Penitentiary, but served a little more than two years before his release in 1898. He returned to his old profession of journalism but was not successful. Some of his stories appeared in the San Francisco *Call*, including a long account of his attempted swindle. He tried to start a magazine, but failed in this. For a while, according to Powell, he lived in the Los Angeles County Poor Farm, but when he died in 1914, he was living in Denver.

The Baroness of Arizona died in the same city in 1934.

With a little luck, he could have become another Mark Hopkins.

16

Who Really Discovered California?

It is unlikely that any country in the world has accumulated a mass of official records and reports that in sheer volume can approach the collection of the Spanish government. The accumulation of papers is the vocation of the bureaucrat, and Spain was a bureaucracy for centuries before John Hancock and his friends began filling the files for the United States. In the Biblioteca Nacional in Madrid and in the Archivo General de las Indias and the files of the Spanish navy in Seville, there are many, many rooms which contain thousands upon thousands of records that have never been examined since the day they first were filed.

The Spanish government is most zealous in protecting this massive accumulation of papers. Ever since the day James Addison Reavis, the self-styled Baron of Arizona, was caught in the act of slipping a forged cedula into the record, there has been a rule, unchanged by civil wars, that any foreign scholar who wishes to study the ancient and dusty papers may do so only in the presence of an armed soldier. In these files are buried the answers to many a secret of the Western World, some of which have been riddles for centuries; others which have been mysteries for only a few years. It was in the Biblioteca Nacional for example that the first clue was uncovered which led to the identification of the enigmatic assassin of the Russian dictator, Leon Trotsky. It was in the Archivo General de las Indias that the first lead was uncovered toward the solution to one of the more puzzling mysteries of the West—the strange disappearance of Captain

159

Francisco de Ulloa in his search for the fabled Seven Cities of Cibola in the Kingdom of Quivira.

Some historians have theorized that Ulloa was stabbed to death while sleeping by one of his disgruntled sailors in Acapulco. Another contends that he died while on an emerald-hunting expedition in Africa. The most logical answer to the centuries-old mystery as to his fate, however, is that he died as a victim of scurvy and dysentery in the San Luis Rey Valley near what is now Oceanside, California. If this is true, and there is strong evidence that it is, then to Ulloa must go the credit for discovering California rather than to Juan Rodríguez Cabrillo, the man generally accepted as the Christopher Columbus of the West Coast.

Ulloa was a key figure in the intrigue, the avarice, and the doublecross that was a way of life among the early political and military leaders of New Spain. Probably the greatest feud of this era was between Antonio de Mendoza, the first viceroy of Mexico, and Hernan Cortes, its conqueror. Subordinates of both men vacillated in their allegiance to each and, if the profits appeared worth the risk, they doublecrossed both with equal aplomb. By early 1539, Cortes and Mendoza were engaged in a frenetic struggle to be the first to loot the incredibly wealthy seven cities of Cibola.

These cities, made of solid gold, were built in the imaginative mind of a Spanish drifter with the improbable name of Cow's Head. Mendoza sent a priest of most dubious reputation, Friar Marcos de Niza, to check on the Cow's Head's story. When the friar returned, he reported to Mendoza that he had been in one of the cities, the smallest of the seven, which was about as large as Mexico City and was indeed built of silver and gold. Although Cortes had described the priest in a letter as a notorious liar, he apparently placed some credence in de Niza's report which was sent to him by spies in the viceroy's castle.

Mendoza made plans to locate the Cibolas with a combination sea and land expedition. The former was headed by a Hernando Alarcón, who was Mendoza's wine tester, and the latter by Francisco Coronado. Mendoza, a phlegmatic man of limited intelligence, had been appointed to his viceregal position because he was one of the favorite courtiers of the king of Spain. Thus he was much more powerful than Cortes but he was no match for his wily rival. His plans for looting the Cibolas were barely out of the discussion stage when Ulloa, working for Cortes, commanding a fleet of three ships, set sail from Acapulco. According to the friar's report, the first of the cities of Cibola was at the head of a navigable stream that emptied into the sea. With a head start of many months, Ulloa should reach the cities well ahead of either of Mendoza's expeditions.

Ulloa left Acapulco on July 8, 1539. In his fleet were the *Santa Agueda,* the *Santo Tomás,* and the *Trinidad.* The ships paused in Colima at the Puerto Santiago de Buena Esperanza where a sailor was put ashore to report back to Cortes on the progress of the voyage. Like Cortes, so did Mendoza have his spies, and the departure of the three ships had not escaped the viceroy's attention. Mendoza's men arrested the messenger and tortured him until he revealed the purpose of the voyage.

Furious, Mendoza ordered a cavalry unit to pursue the ships up the coast and seize all of Cortes' ships and stores. He ordered also that no ships could leave New Spain without his express permission. The unsuspecting Ulloa, meanwhile, ran into a series of storms and put into port at Guatulco, some 360 miles to the north. Here the cavalry unit caught up with him, boarded the *Santo Tomás,* and scuttled it in the harbor. The entire crew and seventeen prostitutes that Ulloa had brought for the comfort of the men were slain. Ulloa escaped with his two other ships.

He continued up the west coast of Mexico to the head of the Gulf of California, searching unsuccessfully for the stream that led to the Cibolas, then down the eastern side of the Baja Peninsula. At La Paz, near the end of the peninsula, he reprovisioned his ships, a port where Mendoza's edict was not yet known. From here he sailed around Cape San Lucas and beat his way to the north. On January 20, 1540, he stopped in a natural harbor at Cedros Island.

It was here that he behaved in a most curious manner. Large, locked caskets which he had carried with him on the *Santa Agueda* were transferred to the smaller *Trinidad.* Officers and men known to be loyal to Cortes were assigned to the *Santa Agueda,* along with the sick, and Ulloa then ordered the ship to return to Acapulco. Ulloa remained behind on board the *Trinidad* with seven of the most attractive prostitutes, a scribe named Pablo Salvador Hernández, another scribe whose name is now unknown, and a crew of twenty-two men. The *Santa Agueda* returned safely to Acapulco, and it is the log of this ship that provides the record of

Ulloa's voyage as far as Cedros Island. What happened to the *Santa Agueda* and the men on board it is unknown. Until very recently, the fate of Ulloa and his *Trinidad* also has been unknown. Other than the two vague references to his death by stabbing in Acapulco or his death on an emerald hunt in Africa, he vanished as thoroughly as Mark Hopkins of New York.

Near the city of Oceanside, California, about thirty-five miles north of San Diego, is the mouth of the San Luis Rey River. It is a rather small stream, both in width and length, extending back from the ocean only a few miles to the San Luis Rey Valley. Here is located the San Luis Rey Mission, a mission in California that is still run by the Franciscans rather than the state. A few centuries ago, the valley was a lake, and the river that drained from it to the ocean was three times as large as it is today.

It was an idyllic spot when the Franciscans built their mission there. The weather was warm the year around, and the land was fertile and verdant. It was inhabited by a large tribe of agrarian Indians who were described by one early Franciscan monk as "so practiced in lewdness and depravity ['would cause Satan to hang his head in shame."

In nearby Oceanside there lives for a few months out of the year a Dr. J. J. Markey, a man sufficiently rich to spend more time on the French Riviera and in Tahiti than on his practice. He is a man with a great sense of curiosity. In 1927, a patient mentioned that there were some petroglyphs on rocks near the edge of the San Luis Rey Valley. The following weekend, Markey rode out on horseback to the area and took pictures of the primitive art. A farmer told him where there were others, and soon the word spread around the San Luis Rey Valley that the doctor had a hobby of photographing petroglyphs.

A few months later another farmer appeared in the offices of Dr. Markey, carrying a cardboard carton. While ploughing, he told Markey, he had turned over an old Indian head in which the doctor might be interested and, opening the box, he rolled out a skull on the doctor's desk. Markey was indeed interested. Not only were there no teeth in the skull, but there were no roots to the teeth in the jaw, and dental problems of this nature were most uncommon to the early Indians. He sent the skull to the University of California at Los Angeles, which verified his suspicions. The skull was about four hundred years old and once had been attached to the body of a European white man who probably had died of scurvy.

This was a disease of old sailors, but four hundred years ago was in 1527 and there were no white European sailors around California at this time. History recorded that the first European to touch land in California was Juan Rodríguez Cabrillo in 1542, and there was no record that his ships had ever put in around the San Luis Rey River. It was a mystery that fascinated the curious doctor. He went to the farmer and with his permission and the help of some Indians he dug in the area where the head had been found, on the banks of where at one time the waters of the lake lapped softly. They found no skeleton, but did unearth a piece of Spanish leathered armor.

Markey found himself obsessed with Spanish History. For a while he could not rid himself of the idea that the skull belonged to one of Cabrillo's sailors who had died and been buried ashore. Then, as now, sailors who died at sea were buried at sea. Cabrillo's voyage was well chronicled, and nowhere was there anything to indicate that he had put ashore anywhere near the San Luis Rey. The doctor turned to other Spanish histories to learn the fate of all Cortes' officers and those of Coronado and Mendoza. Eventually he came across the log of the *Santa Agueda* which told of Ulloa's strange behavior at Cedros Island, a document in the Bancroft Library at the University of California. Markey searched vainly for some further mention of Ulloa, but the only references he could find to the explorer were the two vague references to his death and another which indicated that Ulloa may have testified in a court trial in Spain several years later. Markey placed the mysterious skull on a shelf in his den where it remained as a reminder to still another unsolved riddle of the mysterious West.

In 1951, Markey was in Paris. At a dinner he was introduced to an aristocratic young Spaniard named Miguel de Ulloa. As a conversation piece, Markey mentioned that he once had engaged in considerable research on Francisco de Ulloa and then presently was delighted to learn that his acquaintance was a direct descendant of the Spanish explorer. "Where did he die?" Markey asked casually.

Miguel de Ulloa shrugged. He had only been in the United States once and that was in New York. He did know, however, that Francisco de Ulloa had perished on the same voyage along with all but one of his crew and a scribe.

The reason he knew this, he continued, was a story that he had been told as a youngster of an incredible journey the two survivors had experienced in a longboat, a voyage of more than two thousand miles from somewhere in Alta California to Acapulco. Miguel de Ulloa knew little more, but he did mention to the elated Markey that there was probably some record of this journey by the two survivors in the archives of the Spanish navy in Seville.

Markey abruptly changed his travel plans. Three days later, he was in Seville. He remembered the name of one of the scribes, Pablo Salvador Hernández, and he remembered the year that Ulloa had been left in Cedros Island. In Seville, Markey hired three professional researchers who had the necessary credentials to examine the navy's files. It took the three scholars seven weeks, a very long and expensive seven weeks for Markey, to find the information that the Ocean-side doctor sought. When they did, the results were beyond his wildest expectations. The researchers had found the original report made by Hernández to the commanding officer of the Spanish navy upon his return to Acapulco. It was indeed an incredible story told by Hernández.

Shortly after the *Santa Agueda* left the harbor at Cedros Island for Acapulco, the *Trinidad* did likewise, but headed to the north. Only at this time, Hernández said, did he discover that if Ulloa was successful in locating the Cibolas, he planned to sever all connections with Cortes. It was his plan to strip the Cibolas of all the gold the *Trinidad* could carry, then sail around the Cape to Spain where, after presenting the king his royal fifth, he could live in luxury for the remainder of his life. Ulloa was more concerned with his long voyage to Spain than he was over the possibility that he might not find the Cibolas.

The *Trinidad* sailed north, passed a great natural harbor, explored it, and found it was fed by no river. The ship continued north. About ten leagues above the harbor, it paused at the mouth of a river, but it did not appear navigable. Water from the stream was used to fill the ship's casks. The *Trinidad* passed four large islands but no navigable streams, and eventually Ulloa decided they were too far north for Cibola.

Many members of the crew became ill from dysentery, as were the women on board the ship, and almost all of the crew suffered from scurvy. Ulloa decided to turn back to the river where they had replenished their water supply. The

Trinidad anchored near the mouth of the river. Ulloa ordered Hernández and two members of the crew who were not ill to remain on board the ship. He then opened one of the large caskets, filled a large leather pouch with gold coins, with which to pay the Indians if necessary. From the same source he also paid wages to the crew and the prostitutes.

The first night they set up camp on the shore. The following morning, an exploratory party followed the course of the river back a few miles and discovered that it ended in a lake. Around the lake lived a tribe of Indians who were friendly, provided their visitors with fresh food such as rabbit meat, had never heard of the seven cities of Cibola, and looked upon Ulloa's gold as they did upon the pebbles on the lakeshore. They made no objection when Ulloa set up camp on the side of the lake.

When Hernández visited the camp later, he found about five hundred Indians, all naked and with a ratio of about two females for every male and about five children for each adult. They were extremely dirty, using the lake both as a water supply and a cesspool, and the females constantly were teasing the males into open and public fornication. Hernández and one member of the crew would not drink the water, preferring to slake their thirst with wine of which there was plenty. He was well aware that it was this preference that saved his life.

The camp was set up on August 21, 1540. Two days later, three members of the crew were dead of malignant dysentery, or scurvy, or a combination of both; the scribe did not know. On the third day, Ulloa fell victim to the disease. Others died as the days passed. On August 31, the survivors thought they might escape death by moving away from the Indian camp, and they dragged themselves up a gently sloping hill on the north side of the lake. At the top of the hill was a large cluster of boulders, piled in such a fashion as to form a small cave, and on these rocks some primitive pictures had been etched.

Hernández and the crew member who also only drank wine spent most of their time on the *Trinidad,* but at least on every other day, the scribe would go ashore and hike up the stream to the camp by the cave. On one occasion Ulloa ordered him to bury a large pouch of gold secretly at least two leagues distant from the camp in a place where it would not be found by the Indians. The scribe did as he was ordered, drew a map showing the location of the gold which he gave to Ulloa, then returned to the ship.

The following day a heavy storm struck the area, a storm which lasted for three days, and Hernández did not leave the ship. On the fourth day, he went back to the camp with his companion. Ulloa and the last six members of the crew were dead. The only person in the cave that was alive was one of the prostitutes, but she was dying. Hernández waited until she turned toward the wall, then dropped a large rock on her head to put her out of her misery. He then dragged Ulloa's body out of the cave and, after retrieving the map he had drawn, buried the conquistador on the side of the hill. The other bodies he left inside the cave and covered the entrance with rocks.

Hernández and his companion, who was left unnamed in the report, went back to the *Trinidad*. The ship was much too large to be sailed by a crew of two. Their only chance of survival was to try to reach civilization in the *Trinidad's* long boat.

There is no mention in Hernández' report of the size of the longboat, but it must have been a pitifully small vessel, as the *Trinidad*, which carried it, was a ship of only twenty tons. There is no further mention of the caskets of treasure that Ulloa had transferred from the *Santa Agueda* to his quarters on the *Trinidad* and what could have been the most dramatic account of the scribe's report is told only in the most terse language, yet the two men *rowed* a distance of approximately two thousand miles down the coast of Alta and Baja California and then across the open sea to Acapulco. Nor is any mention made as to how they were received upon their arrival.

The researchers hired by Markey gave him photographic copies of the report and the map attached to the report, which gave the location of the buried coins. Another crude map showed where Hernández had left the *Trinidad* at anchor. There also was a brief enigmatic notation on the report that Hernández died in 1571 and an English translation of the document.

With the papers in his possession, Markey flew home where he immediately rounded up six members of the San Luis Rey Historical Society, an organization that he had helped found in 1932, and set forth on a new round of exploration of the San Luis Rey Valley.

The only spot that answered the description of the boulders with the primitive etchings was the same cluster of rocks that displayed the petroglyphs Markey had studied a quarter of a century earlier. The cave to which Hernández referred was located one league due north of these rocks in an escarpment. It took Markey three days to find the cave entrance. It was located under a heavy growth of scrub oak, and the opening had been clogged with smaller rocks and stones which Markey finally was able to loosen with a pick-axe. They covered an opening about two and one half feet tall and five feet wide. Markey eased himself into the aperture and let himself down into a small cave about twenty feet long and fifteen feet across. Lying on the floor of the cave were seven skeletons. Six of them were male. One, considerably smaller, was that of a female, and the skull was badly crushed.

It took more than six years, however, to find the coins that Hernández buried. The terrain had changed drastically. The lake had shrunk to the size of a reed filled pond. Two leagues was a distance of approximately six miles, and there was always the question as to whether or not Hernández had followed Ulloa's instructions literally. The search continued regularly and finally was justified in September of 1957 when a metal detector buzzed on the ground at a point a little more than seven miles distant from the burial cave. The treasure was buried very close to the surface, some two thousand coins inside the rotted remnants of leather bags. The coins were dated from 1500 A.D. back to the Roman Empire of the first century. They have been valued by collectors at more than $250,000. One coin alone weighs more than a pound.

Was Ulloa the first European to discover California? The evidence certainly seems to indicate that this is so. Markey is convinced that this is the case, but he wants one more piece of evidence that would prove his theory beyond any argument. Somewhere on the bottom of the sea, probably between Oceanside and San Diego, lie the remains of the *Trinidad*. It carries a great treasure, if Hernández' account is correct, and he was in telling of the graves and the buried coins. In addition, there is a reward of $10,000 from the San Luis Rey Historical Society to the first scuba diver who finds the wreckage.

The credit for discovering California now is accorded to Juan Rodríguez Cabrillo who, a little more than two years later, flying the flag of the Viceroy Mendoza, sailed up the west coast of Alta California. Like Ulloa, Cabrillo never returned to Mexico, and there are many mysterious circumstances surrounding his death and his "burial on the lonely San Miguel Island off the coast of California."

17

The King of San Miguel

Lying some thirty miles south of Point Concepcion in California is San Miguel Island. Shaped roughly like a triangle, it is approximately nine miles long and four and one half miles wide at its largest point in the middle.

Technically, it does not belong to the United States, despite its geographical location approximately two hundred miles north of the Mexican border. None of the so-called Channel Islands were mentioned in the treaty under which the United States acquired California from Mexico, a point which is brought up at regular intervals by Mexican politicians. The State Department never has debated the matter seriously with our southern neighbors, but with the exception of Santa Catalina Island, it is doubtful if anyone really cares about the title.

San Miguel is the most mysterious of the eight channel islands. It is a barren, windswept land, haunted by ghosts of prehistoric tribes, and there is a legend that any male who attempts to make it his home is doomed to die violently. Much has happened there to support the legend.

One of the strangest and most persistent myths about San Miguel is that it marks the burial spot for Juan Rodríguez Cabrillo, who probably was the second conquistador to sail up the west coast of California. This legend, so prevalent that it is taught in California schools as fact, contends that Cabrillo discovered the island in October of 1542, and that during his exploration of it he fell and broke his arm. He sailed on to what is now Monterey, where gangrene or blood poisoning developed from his injury. The sorrowing crew

169

took him back to La Posesion, his name for the island, where he died and was buried on January 3, 1543. His grave has never been found, but a monument to the explorer was erected by members of the Cabrillo Civic Clubs of California and dedicated on January 3, 1937 on a section of the island known as Dead Man's Point which overlooks Cuyler Bay on the northern side. The monument now is mottled with lichen, a tall granite cross set in a mount of cemented lava rock. Its inscription reads:

> JOÃO RODRIGUEZ CABRILLO
> Discoverer of California
> Isle of Burial — 1543

As a memorial, it is futile. Years pass with no one on the island to read the inscription and, according to the testimony at a Spanish Court of Inquiry investigating the explorer's death, this was not the island on which the explorer was buried. The story of Cabrillo's death can be traced to an old chronicle of the voyage written by a Juan Paez. There were, however, three "Juan Paezes" of that era, all of whom were writers. One was an *escribano publico* who lived in Guatemala and was known to be a personal friend of the explorer's. Another was a João Pais, a conquistador who wrote some memoirs of his experiences in Mexico, and the third was Juan Paez de Castro, named by the king of Spain as that nation's official historian, but who never got past the prologue to his monumental work and was never known to have left Spain. None of the three accompanied Cabrillo on his voyage, nor is it known which of the three wrote the fictional account of Cabrillo's death.

The testimony at the Court of Inquiry into Cabrillo's death, offered by his three senior officers, Lázaro de Cárdenas, Lorenzo Hernández, and Bartolomé Ferrer, told a different story. Long after departing from La Posesion, or San Miguel, they came to an island near the 45th parallel which Cabrillo named *La Capitana*. A detail was put ashore to search for water and was attacked on the beach by a band of hostile Indians. Cabrillo, coming to their rescue, slipped as he leaped for a rock on the shore, breaking his leg and crushing the shin bone. It was from this injury that he fell victim to gangrene, and it was at La Capitana that he died and was buried about ten days later. The 45th parallel runs through the State of Oregon, and it is open to speculation

as to which island in this area was named La Capitana by
Cabrillo. The names have been changed many times, and
there is no island on the 45th parallel.

San Miguel was given its present name by a Miguel Cos-
tanso, a cartographer who drew a coastal map of land he
had never seen, but renamed the island after his name saint.
It is one of the most treacherous areas along the western
coast of the United States.

Among the wrecks known to have gone down on the west
side of the island is a Spanish Manila galleon which carried
more than $2 million worth of gold coin. Its location is
known, but thus far, no one has been able to reach it. A
scuba diver would be battered to death immediately by the
constant breakers, and no vessel would be able to hover over
it. Other ships which have fallen prey to the hostile island
include the *San Sebastian*, which sank in 1754, the *J. F.
West*, which smashed against the shore in 1889, the *Comet*
in 1911, and the *Cuba* in 1923. Even the natural harbor
offers no reliable sanctuary. Today, twisted steel girders and
rusted mooring hooks are all that remain of a small pier
built by its last known inhabitants.

The legend of the island holds that it has been cursed
since Cabrillo met his fate there. Although evidence indicates that Cabrillo did not die here, there have been many
strange happenings on San Miguel Island which could give
credence to such a curse. At irregular intervals, searchers
for the alleged Cabrillo grave have unearthed other skeletons. Some have been dated back long before the arrival of
the conquistadores, and they are not the bones of Indians.
Another unconfirmed report concerns the skeleton of a
young woman found lying on the ground near Crook Point.
Nylon stockings encased the bony legs, fastened to a garter
belt around the spine. No one knows who she was nor how
she could have reached such a desolate area.

During the administration of President Grover Cleveland,
a man known only as Captain Waters claimed San Miguel
as his independent domain. As Mexico has asserted, so did
Waters, the Channel Islands are not a part of the United
States since they were not specifically mentioned in the
Treaty of Guadalupe Hidalgo. Waters challenged Cleveland
or any other member of the United States government to
prove that San Miguel had been acquired legally by the U.S.

The florid captain mailed his claim to Washington from
Santa Barbara, then sailed on his short voyage to his newly

found kingdom. A few days later, the U.S. Navy dispatched a small warship to the island where they found Waters' small sloop at anchor in Cuyler Harbor. A Navy detail spent more than a week searching the island for Captain Waters, but could find no trace of him. The search was abandoned.

Approximately a month later, an early fall storm swept in from the Pacific. When it subsided, a fishing trawler spotted Waters' sloop drifting in the Santa Barbara Channel and towed it into San Pedro. The sails were furled, and the vessel appeared to be in the same condition as when last seen by the Navy detachment. The island again was searched for Waters, but there was no sign of him. There never has been.

San Miguel's longest and its last inhabitant died violently in 1942 after spending fourteen peaceful years on the island with his wife and two daughters who were born there. His name was Herbert C. Lester, and he called himself the King of San Miguel.

Before moving to his kingdom, Lester was a brilliant New Yorker, a member of the Union League Club. His brother, a prominent New York attorney, at one time was a member of the New York State Legislature. The "King" became fed up with civilization in 1928 and brought his bride of three weeks to the isolated island. She also came from a prominent American family, a direct descendant of Roger Sherman who signed the Declaration of Independence and later became governor of Connecticut.

During his fourteen-year reign, the King left the island only three or four times and his trip was no farther than Santa Barbara. Once a year, however, a supply boat would arrive with its annual supply of staples and a tremendous number of books. The two children, Marianne and Betsy, were educated by their mother. His castle was a large, triangular-shaped building constructed from the wreckage of the *J. F. West* and the medium-sized pine trees that are found on the island.

In 1942, the Kingdom of San Miguel came to an abrupt end. The U.S. Navy served notice on Lester that the island had been designated as a Navy bombing range, and that Lester and his family would have to move back to civilization. The King remonstrated, but to no avail. On June 19, 1942, at the age of fifty-four, he shot himself to death in his well-stocked library. His grieving family buried him on a section of the island known as Devil's Knoll, a site opposite

Dead Man's Point at the west end of the crescent-shaped Cuyler Harbor. His wife and daughters moved back to the United States.

The house that he built still stands, despite the heavy bombing the island received during the war. To reach it today, one must cross a large pocket of quicksand, then scale a three-hundred-foot sandswept hill peppered with fossil forests and kitchen middens. The "castle" is perched near the end of a steep grass canyon, and near the house a windmill still may churn idly. There is a pumphouse with rusted equipment inside and rolling away from the building is an immense sweep of lush grazing land enclosed by rotted posts. Near one section of the fence are more than one hundred sheep skulls, shielded from the wind by lava rock, and piled neatly in the manner of the skulls at the Catacombs.

The inside of the house remains furnished as it was on the day the King died. The mattresses on the beds and the stuffing for the furniture has rotted and decayed. The many hundreds of books left behind are moldy. In the binding of one book, located in a floor to ceiling bookcase, there is a bullet hole.

It is unlikely that more than a dozen persons have gone to San Miguel Island since the family of the dead King abandoned it. None has remained overnight. No one has touched anything, possibly for the fear of invoking the curse of San Miguel. The sheep run wild, and there are many varieties of small game.

Not long ago, the U.S. Navy announced that it plans once again to use San Miguel Island as a practice bombing range. This time it may run into more formidable opposition than it did when it overthrew the kingdom of Herbert C. Lester in 1942. The island does not belong to the United States. It belongs to Mexico, in spite of its location some 250 miles north of the land border between the two nations. In 1942, Mexico was a wartime ally of the United States, and in allowing the use of San Miguel as a bombing range, it was cooperating in the war effort.

The situation no longer is the same. If the Navy capriciously starts bombing San Miguel, a portion of a neighboring nation, it could be construed as an act of unprovoked aggression.

Epilogue

There is a story told about the young man from Boston who was visiting the Olympia Yacht Club on the lower end of Puget Sound in the Pacific Northwest.

After a pleasant afternoon of sailing and during a tall cool drink on the sundeck, the subject turned to gweducs and of the delightful sport in catching them.

"What kind of ducks?" the Bostonian asked curiously.

"G-w-e-d-u-c-s is the way the dictionary spells them," he was told, "but most people around the Sound just call them gooey ducks."

The stranger nodded and smiled. "I see," he said. "How do you catch them?"

"You need a length of stovepipe and a shovel. You see, a gooey duck is really a very large clam that is found around this area. Its neck is between four and five feet long. It has a shell at least a half-foot in diameter, and each will weigh anywhere from eight to ten pounds."

The Bostonian entered into the spirit of the conversation. "Tomorrow morning," he said, leaning back in his chair, "I will get myself a shovel and a piece of stovepipe. Should the stovepipe be painted a bright color or is something more conservative in better taste?"

"We're serious," he was told. "You see, the gooey duck burrows into the sand at low tide. If he has a six-foot neck, he will burrow that deep. When he hears you coming, he pulls in his neck and hopes that you won't see him in six feet of sand. That's why you need a stovepipe."

Again the Bostonian nodded and smiled. "Now after you've caught this monster, what do you do with him?" he asked politely.

"His neck is best in chowder and the rest usually is sliced into thick steaks. There is probably no better eating in the State of Washington."

"And is gooey-duck hunting on the agenda?" the Bostonian asked.

His companions looked at each other and nodded. "We have a low tide tomorrow morning about four," one replied. "Would you like to come?"

"I wouldn't miss such an adventure for the world," the easterner asserted. "Where shall I meet you?"

His host named a point on the beach about a mile distant.

"I'll see you there," said the stranger.

But the Bostonian was not on the beach at four the following morning. He knew better than to be the butt of such a broad practical joke.

All of his companions at the yacht club, however, were on the beach, each carrying a shovel and a length of stovepipe . . . because everything they had told him was true.

It is wise to believe a little bit in everything.

ABOUT THE AUTHORS

Brad Williams was born in New York City, and raised in Massachusetts. He has worked for AP, UP and INS and various newspapers in various locations ranging from Portland, Oregon and Los Angeles, California, to Mexico, D. F. and New Delhi, India. Mr. Williams has published several mystery novels and nonfiction works; his books include *Flight 967* and *Due Process.*

Choral Pepper is the former editor of "Desert Magazine." She has also worked as an interior designer, Las Vegas show reviewer, columnist and free-lance writer. She has traveled extensively, both abroad and in the United States, and has written two previously published books, the most recent of which is *Zodiac Parties.*